Blueprint INTERMEDIATE

Students' Book

Brian Abbs
Ingrid Freebairn

Longman

Contents

Introducing Nick		**7**	

Unit 1 Nick · 8
A schoolboy at Eton

Vocabulary	Word field: education
	Word stress: education
Listening	Opinions on education
Talking point	For and against schools like Eton

Unit 2 Grammar · 10
Present simple and continuous

Listening	Advertisement for TV series
Writing	Character description

Unit 3 Communication · 12
Shopping

Dialogue	Buying a record
Act it out	Shopping situations
Listening	Conversation: shopping in a record shop
Writing	Dialogue in a record shop

Unit 4 Grammar · 14
Not supposed to/not allowed to

Dialogue	Outside a theatre
Writing	Restrictions and rules
Listening	Theatre announcement

Unit 5 Reading · 15
Understanding boys

Vocabulary	Adjectives describing people and their opposites
Writing	Linking devices: *both . . . and, as well as, neither . . . nor . . .*

Unit 6 Grammar · 16
Past simple and continuous

Listening	Narrative: account of a theft
Writing	Narrative: account of recent incident

Unit 7 Topic · 18
Living at home

Reading	A room of my own
Vocabulary	Adverb formation with *-ly*
	Word stress: adjectives and adverbs
Listening	Narrative with time connectors: an amusing incident
Writing	Time connectors: *after, at the age of, during, when, eventually, now, for a time* Autobiography/biography

Unit 8 Communication · 20
Apologies

Dialogue	Father and daughter arguing
Listening	Conversation: apologies at a party
Writing	Letter of thanks and apology

Unit 9 Grammar · 22
Used to/be used to

Act it out	Conversation about a university student
Listening	Students' opinions of life in Britain
Writing	Informal letter: settling down in a foreign country Linking devices: *another thing is, also*

Unit 10 Reading · 24
Cider with Rosie

Style	Similes
Talking point	For and against growing up in a large family
Vocabulary	Compound nouns: furniture and fittings
	Word stress: compound nouns
Writing	Guided composition: description of an interesting room

Self check 1 · 26
Units 1–10

Fluency 1 · 28
A study trip to Britain

Introducing Angie 29

Unit 11 Angie 30
A motorcycle courier

Vocabulary	Word field: jobs and professions
	Noun formation: suffixes *-er, -or, -ist*
	Word stress: jobs and professions
Talking point	Sex roles and work
About Britain	London's Docklands
Listening	Monologue: social changes in the Docklands

Unit 12 Grammar 32
Future tenses: *going to/will*

Listening	Telephone conversation: making arrangements
Writing	Message for noticeboard

Unit 13 Communication 34
Requests

Dialogue	Receptionist and courier
Writing	Note to a teacher: explanation and request
Listening	Telephone request from a client
Act it out	Conversation with a taxi driver

Unit 14 Grammar 36
Ability and possibility: *can/could/be able to*

Act it out	Conversation between parent and son/daughter who wants to work abroad
Writing	Letter: invitation and arrangements

Unit 15 Reading 38
Hidden London

Talking point	For and against guided tours
Vocabulary	Adjective formation: prefix *-un*
Writing	Tour programme

Unit 16 Grammar 40
First conditional and time clauses

Listening	Radio interview with athletics trainer
Writing	List of Do's and Don'ts for sports

Unit 17 Topic 42
Sport

Reading	The Olympic Games
Vocabulary	Word field: sports and sports locations
	Word stress: compound nouns
Listening	Sports commentaries
Talking point	For and against holding the Olympic Games in your country
Writing	Letter of protest to a newspaper

Unit 18 Communication 44
Checking Information

Dialogue	Angie and a young neighbour
Listening	Conversation: in the street
Act it out	Meeting a new acquaintance in the street
Reading	When is a question not a question?
Writing	Paragraph about difficulties in learning English. Linking devices: *another reason is, also, and finally*

Unit 19 Grammar 46
In case

Talking point	Travel precautions
Listening	Person giving advice about travel precautions
Writing	Note of welcome and explanation

Unit 20 Reading 47
The Loneliness of the Long-distance Runner

Talking point	Punishment for young criminals
Style	Sentence length
Vocabulary	Phrasal verbs with *run*

Self check 2 48
Units 11–20

Fluency 2 50
Holiday Roundabout

Introducing Glenn 51

Unit 21 Glenn 52
An American in Britain

Vocabulary	The verb *to get* + adjective/past participle
	Different pronunciations of *ea*
Listening	Impressions of Stratford
Talking point	Effects of tourism

Unit 22 Grammar 54
Present perfect simple and continuous

Listening	Letter cassette: personal news
Writing	Informal letter-writing expressions
	Informal letter: personal news

Unit 23 Communication 56
Making complaints

Dialogue	Waiter and restaurant customers
Listening	Telephone conversations: making complaints and requesting action
Reading	Extracts from a mail order catalogue
	A letter of complaint
Writing	Formal letter of complaint

Unit 24 Grammar 58
Make/do

Writing	Sentences: discriminating between *make* and *do*

Unit 25 Reading 59
Hamlet, Prince of Denmark

Vocabulary	Word field: the theatre
Writing	Composition: the story of a play or novel

Unit 26 Grammar 60
The passive

Listening	Description of an audition
Writing	Informal letter from listening notes

Unit 27 Topic 62
The USA

Reading	The Empire State Building
Vocabulary	Word field: Types of buildings
Listening	Opinions of the USA
Writing	Composition: description of a famous monument or landmark

Unit 28 Communication 64
Obligation and prohibition

About Britain	Table manners
Talking point	Polite behaviour
Act it out	Conversation about a special social event
Listening	Table manners in the USA
Writing	Paragraphs: useful information for foreigners about etiquette

Unit 29 Grammar 66
Defining relative pronouns

Writing	Descriptive paragraph using defining relative pronouns

Unit 30 Reading 68
How to be an alien

Vocabulary	Adjective formation: suffixes *-less* and *-ful*
Listening	Discussion: national stereotypes portrayed in jokes
Talking point	Views of the British
Writing	Paragraphs discussing national stereotypes
	Contrasting devices: *in fact, but, actually*

Self check 3 70
Units 21–30

Fluency 3 72
Celebration time

Introducing Eve   73

Unit 31 Eve   74
A jewellery maker

About Britain	Avebury
Vocabulary	Word field: jewellery and parts of body
	Pronunciation: words ending in -*ough*
Listening	A silversmith talks about his work
Talking point	The most important aspects of a job
Writing	Paragraph: justifying job choice
	Linking devices: *the main reason, another good reason, besides*

Unit 32 Grammar   76
Second conditional *if* clauses

Reading	Assertiveness questionnaire
Act it out	Being assertive
Talking point	Choosing a perfect occupation
Listening	Discussion: perfect occupations

Unit 33 Communication   78
Polite requests for information

Dialogue	Eve makes a phone call
Act it out	Asking for information
Listening	Radio interview with a yachtsman
Writing	Newspaper article
About Britain	Phone cards

Unit 34 Grammar   80
Have/get something done

Dialogue	In a garage
Listening	Complaint in a TV rental shop
Reading	Opinions of the British telephone system
Talking point	The telephone system
Writing	Linking devices: *whereas*
	Paragraph comparing life in two countries

Unit 35 Reading   82
Competitive women

Listening	Discussion: 'traditional' and 'modern' business people
Vocabulary	Dictionary definitions

Unit 36 Grammar   83
Past modal verbs: *should have/ought to have*

Talking point	Assigning blame after a road accident
Writing	Critical letter on football hooliganism

Unit 37 Topic   84
Ethics

Reading	How far does friendship go?
Vocabulary	Verb and adjective formation from nouns
	Word stress: words ending in -*ion* and -*ity*
Listening	A personal dilemma
Writing	Linking devices: *however*
	Sentences: contrasting ideas

Unit 38 Communication   86
Explanation and clarification

Dialogue	Student and mother discussing application form
Writing	Letter of application for a job
Listening	Conversation during college registration

Unit 39 Grammar   88
Past modal verbs: *could have/might have/must have/can't have*

Dialogue	Friends waiting outside a cinema
Act it out	Telephone conversation with a friend
Writing	Formal letter: enquiry about a missing item
Listening	An account of a mugging

Unit 40 Reading   90
Gather Together in My Name

Style	Similes and metaphors
Writing	A biographical extract

Self check 4   92
Units 31–40

Fluency 4   94
International food festival

Introducing Errol   95

Unit 41 Errol   96
A police officer

Vocabulary	World field and derivation: crimes and criminals
	Word stress: compound nouns
Talking point	Police and their image
Listening	A police officer discusses her work

Unit 42 Grammar   98
Reported speech (1)
Statements and questions

Dialogue	Reporting a missing briefcase to the police
Writing	Report: missing briefcase

Unit 43 Communication   100
Closing strategies

Dialogue 1	In the office
Dialogue 2	In a supermarket
Listening	Closing exchanges
Act it out	Telephone conversation with a friend
Writing	Informal letter: emphasis on letter endings

Unit 44 Grammar   102
Reported speech (2)
Verbs of reporting

Listening	Conversation: a broken arrangement
Writing	Informal letter: reporting a broken arrangement
Act it out	Conversation with a friend about a visit to a nightclub

Unit 45 Reading   104
The changing role of the police

Vocabulary	Prepositions after verbs
Listening	News report: violent behaviour

Unit 46 Grammar   105
Past perfect simple

Listening	Conversation: account of an unfortunate incident
Writing	Composition: report from notes on listening

Unit 47 Topic   106
Mysteries and thrillers

Reading	Agatha Christie disappears
Vocabulary	World field: types of books
Talking point	What makes a good thriller?
Writing	Linking devices: *although, in spite of*
	Paragraphs about a thriller

Unit 48 Communication   108
Expressing regrets

Dialogue	Conversation in an office
Listening	A young person regretting past decisions
Writing	A short story about a regret
Talking point	Regret about changes around you

Unit 49 Grammar   110
Third conditional *if* clauses

Dialogue	Parking in the wrong place
Listening	Conversation: an unusual robbery
Talking point	What would you have done?
Reading	Newspaper item
Writing	News item based on a headline

Unit 50 Reading   112
A Judgement in Stone

Listening	Radio panel discussion
Talking point	Coping with dyslexia
Style	Dramatic effect: sentences without main verbs
Vocabulary	Adverb formation from adjectives
	Second syllable stress in adverbs
Writing	Punctuation of novel
	Continuation of the story

Self check 5   114
Units 41–50

Fluency 5   116
Pupils in terror ride

Grammar index   117
Communication Index   120
Vocabulary list   122
Self check keys   125

Introducing Nick

Look at the pictures of Nick.
How old do you think he is?
What's his school uniform like?
What sort of school does he go to?
Do you think he enjoys it?
What do you think he wants to do with his life?

Now read about Nick. Were you right?

—1—
Nick

A schoolboy at Eton

'I know I should feel privileged being here at Eton. It's costing my father a fortune in fees, as he keeps telling me. But actually, I think it can be a handicap in life to go to a school like Eton. People think we're arrogant and snobbish, with no brains or talent.

'All right, so I'm not particularly brainy. I'm not the academic type. I don't want to go to university. I want to be a musician. At the moment I'm making a 'demo' tape to send round to record companies and it's really annoying my old man.'

Nick Harrington is eighteen and in his final year at Eton College. He's taking three 'A' levels this summer in Maths, Physics and Computer Studies. However, his teachers are not happy with his work. They think he's spending too much time playing his guitar and reading music magazines.

Nick has his own room at Eton where he sleeps and studies. He goes home for the weekend twice a term but otherwise doesn't get much freedom.

'We're allowed to go into town in the afternoons but we're not supposed to go into pubs. And we're certainly not allowed out of school after six o'clock in the evening. Last term the headmaster sent two boys home for a week because they met some girls in a pub. I think that's ridiculous. Anyway, I don't really care any more. I'm leaving school at the end of term and then I can do what I like.'

Glossary
quaint unusual, slightly old-fashioned
'demo' demonstration
old man (coll) father

Words to learn
privileged   fortune   fees   handicap
arrogant   brains   academic   annoy
otherwise   freedom   ridiculous   afford

Eton College
Eton College is the top public school for boys in the United Kingdom. The quaint title 'public' means exactly the opposite of what it says, for most children cannot go to this type of school. The fees for public schools are so high that only very few people can afford to send their children there. Private education of this kind exists in no other country on the same scale.

UNIT 1: Nick

1 Read and answer.
1 Why should Nick feel privileged to be at Eton?
2 Why does he think it's a handicap to go there?
3 Why are his teachers not pleased with him?
4 Why did the headmaster send two boys home?

2 Read and think.
1 Why do you think Nick's parents wanted him to go to Eton?
2 What do you think Nick's relationship with his father is like?
3 What do you think Nick doesn't like about Eton?

3 About you
1 Was your school like Eton in any way?
2 Are there many private schools in your country?
3 What sort of people go to these schools?

VOCABULARY
1 In pairs, discuss the difference in meaning between the following:

private/state school   day/boarding school
primary/secondary school   to go to college/to get into college
to take/pass/fail an exam   to get a pass/good grade/degree

2 Listen to how the following are stressed.

DAY school   STATE school   PRImary school
BOARDing school

Write the words below with the correct stress in capital letters. Then say them aloud.

night school   private school   evening class
public school   English class

3 Use some of the words and phrases from Vocabulary Exercises 1 and 2 to write about your own education.

LISTENING
Before you listen
Look at the statements on the right. Which ones indicate that the speaker   a) approves of   b) disapproves of schools like Eton?

Listen
Three other people give their opinions of public schools like Eton. Listen and note whether the speaker approves or disapproves of these schools.

TALKING POINT
In groups, talk about the advantages and disadvantages of going to a school like Eton, using the expressions below.

Giving an opinion	Agreeing	Disagreeing
I think (that) . . .	So/Nor do I.	Oh, I don't./Oh, I do.
I honestly think (that) . . .	I agree.	I'm not sure I agree.
I don't think (that) . . .	I think you're right.	I really don't agree.
		I disagree.

1 'I think all private education is unfair.'

2 'I'd like to go to Eton if I could be sure of getting better 'A' level grades there.'

3 'People who go to public schools are snobs. They think they're better than anyone else.'

4 'I don't think there's anything wrong in paying for your education.'

5 'I honestly think they have no idea how anyone lives in the real world.'

–2–

Grammar

Present simple and continuous

What's the difference in meaning?

1 Nick plays the guitar.
2 Nick is playing the guitar.

Which verb tense is used in each sentence? Look back at the text about Nick in Unit 1. How many different examples of the two tenses can you find? Is each tense always used in the same way? Check the Focus section below to see the different ways in which the two tenses are used.

FOCUS

The present simple

This tense is used

- to talk about general facts which are true most or all of the time:
  Nick has his own room at Eton.

- to talk about routine or frequency:
  He goes home twice a term.

- with verbs of emotion, e.g. *like, love, hate, want*:
  I don't want to go to university.

- with verbs of thinking, e.g. *think, know, understand*:
  I think it can be a handicap to go to a school like Eton.

The present continuous

This tense is used

- to talk about events which are happening now or around the time of speaking:
  I'm making a 'demo' tape.

- to talk about definite arrangements in the future:
  He's taking three 'A' levels this summer.

- When referring to the future, the tense occurs particularly with verbs like *go, come, see, visit, meet, arrive* and *leave*, which are often connected with timetables and diary arrangements:
  He's leaving on Friday.

Note
The present continuous is not generally used with verbs of emotion and thinking.

PRACTICE

1 Use the text about Nick in Unit 1 to write questions for these answers.

EXAMPLE
1 He goes to Eton.
  Where does Nick go to school?

2 He thinks it can be a handicap in life to go there.
3 No, he doesn't. He wants to be a musician.
4 He likes playing his guitar and reading music magazines.
5 Maths, Physics and Computer Studies.
6 Twice a term.
7 At the end of term.

2 Look at the chart on the right. Ask and answer about Nick, Beth and Tom. Use the present simple or present continuous tense.

EXAMPLES
A: Where does Nick live?
B: He lives with his parents near London.

A: Apart from 'A' levels, what else is he doing at the moment?
B: He's making a 'demo' tape.

3 Interview your partner and make a similar chart. After the interview, close your notebooks and tell the class as much as you can remember about your partner.

UNIT 2: Grammar

LISTENING

Listen to an announcement for a new TV soap opera about a theatre family called 'The Hartleys'.
Draw a family tree for the Hartley family and then write at least one fact about each person.

EXAMPLE
Charles is a famous actor.

WRITING

1 Before you write

Look at the picture below and read the paragraph about Nick's father.

Rex Harrington is Nick's father. He is a rich businessman of about forty-five. He's tall and dark. He wears dark suits but at weekends he wears casual clothes. He usually gets up at six, does some exercises and then goes to the office. He never gets back before ten o'clock at night so he doesn't see much of his family. He is interested in collecting pictures of horses. At the moment he is travelling on business in America because he's opening an office over there next year.

2 Use the text about Nick's father as a model to write about someone you know.

Say what they do and how old they are. Describe what they look like and what sort of clothes they wear. Describe part of their daily routine and what their interests are. Finish by describing their current activities, future plans and ambitions. Link your sentences with *and, but, then, so* and *because*. Include some time markers like *at the moment*.

3 Now write about yourself in the same way.

NICK
Home with parents near London
Favourite magazine New Musical Express
Favourite food steak and chips
Interests playing the guitar
Exams 'A' level Maths, Physics, Computer Studies
Current activity making a 'demo' tape
Ambition to be a musician

BETH
Home small village near Bath
Favourite magazine The Face
Favourite food pasta
Interests reading
Exams 'A' level English, History, Economics
Current activity learning to drive
Ambition to be a journalist

TOM
Home with parents in Reading
Favourite magazine The Biker
Favourite food Indian Food
Interests cycling
Exams 'A' level Portuguese, Spanish, English
Current activity training for the Round Britain Cycle Race
Ambition to be a travel courier

—3—

Communication

Shopping

Look at the photograph above and answer the questions.

1 Where is Nick?
2 What is he buying?
3 How much does an LP or music cassette cost in your country?

🔊 DIALOGUE

NICK: Excuse me, have you got the latest Simply Red album?
ASSISTANT: No, I'm afraid we've completely sold out.
NICK: Oh, pity. Do you have *Greatest Hits on The Guitar*?
ASSISTANT: Yes, I think it's in stock. One moment and I'll check.
NICK: Thanks.
ASSISTANT: Yes, here we are.
NICK: Great. How much is it?
ASSISTANT: £6.99.
NICK: O.K. I'll have it.
ASSISTANT: Right. Here's your receipt.
NICK: Thanks.

Listen and answer the questions.

1 Which albums does Nick ask for?
2 Which one does he buy?
3 How much is it?
4 Why couldn't he buy the other one?

FOCUS
Shopping

- Asking for things:
  Have you got the latest Simply Red album?
  Have you got any records by Simply Red?
  Do you have Picture Book by Simply Red?

- Saying if things are not available:
  I'm afraid we've sold out.
  I'm afraid it's not in stock.
  I'm afraid we haven't got any at the moment.

- Deciding to buy:
  Thanks, I'll have it (them).
  Yes, I'll take this one (these), please.
  I think I'll have this one (these), please.

- Deciding not to buy:
  I think I'll leave it, thank you.
  Thanks, but it's (they're) not quite what I want.

Note
When deciding to buy or not to buy, *have* and *take* are interchangeable. *Buy* is rarely used.

UNIT 3: Communication

PRACTICE

1 Act out conversations.

You have a list of things to buy in a stationery shop. The shop assistant has prices and details of what is available in the shop. Sometimes the item you want will not be available so you must decide whether to buy an alternative item or not. In pairs, practise several conversations changing parts.

CUSTOMER'S LIST
Tina Turner's Greatest Hits

The Rats by James Herbert
Airmail writing paper
Coloured marker pens

Beat magazine

ASSISTANT'S NOTES
Tina Turner's Greatest Hits: sold out
All paperback books £2.50
Writing paper: airmail £1.75
Coloured marker pens 46p each. Only red and green.
Magazines in stock: *Vogue* £2, *Arena* £1.50
Sold out: *Hondo, Beat, Mizz*

Start like this:
CUSTOMER: Excuse me. Have you got *Tina Turner's Greatest Hits*?
ASSISTANT: No, I'm afraid we . . .

2 In pairs, use the dialogue and the pictures below to shop for clothes.

CUSTOMER: Excuse me, can I try this jacket on?
ASSISTANT: Yes, of course.
(a few minutes later)
Any good?

C: Yes, it's fine. How much is it?
A: It's £79.99.
C: Yes, I think I'll have it, please.
A: Fine, I'll put it in a bag.

C: No, I'm afraid it's not quite what I want. I think I'll leave it, thank you.
A: O.K.

LISTENING

Before you listen

1 Name as many different types of music as you can.
2 What else, apart from records, can you buy in a big music and record store?
3 What different ways can you pay for goods in a shop?

Listen to the conversation in a record shop.

Note down:
the two things the customer came to buy.
why she did not buy them.
what she finally bought.
what they cost and how she paid.

WRITING

Write a dialogue. You are in a record shop and you ask an assistant if she's got a particular record or cassette. She says she hasn't and gives a reason. You then ask about another record. When she brings it, ask how much it costs. Decide if you are or are not going to buy it.

£22.25

£79.99

£36.65

£69.99

£9.99

13

4

Grammar

Not allowed to and not supposed to

🔊 DIALOGUE

One Saturday afternoon, Nick passes a crowd of people outside the Theatre Royal, Windsor.

NICK: Hello, Alex.
ALEX: Oh, hi Nick!
NICK: What's happening?
ALEX: We're waiting to see Timothy Dalton. I want to get his autograph.
NICK: Why don't you go in?
ALEX: We're not allowed to. We have to wait until he comes out.
MAN: Come on, you lot, move on. You know you're not supposed to block the street.
ALEX: Here he is!

Later

ALEX: Well at least I got his autograph! Do you want to come and have a coffee?
NICK: O.K. but it'll have to be quick. I'm supposed to be revising.

Listen and answer the questions.

1 Why are the girls waiting outside the theatre?
2 Why can't they go in?
3 Why is the doorman irritated?
4 What does Alex invite Nick to do?
5 Why does Nick say: 'It'll have to be quick'?

FOCUS

'Not allowed to'
- This is used when the speaker is giving a definite rule:
  We're not allowed to go in the theatre.

'Not supposed to'
- This is often used when talking about a rule which people sometimes break.
  You're not supposed to block the street.

Note
In the positive: *allowed to* = have permission to, but *supposed to* = have an obligation to i.e. it is expected behaviour.

Look back at the text about Nick in Unit 1 and find examples of (*not*) *allowed to* and (*not*) *supposed to*.

PRACTICE

1 Write restrictions and rules for the following places or situations.

EXAMPLE
1 In an aeroplane you're not allowed to smoke in the toilets. You're not supposed to stand up until the plane comes to a complete halt.

1 in an aeroplane
2 in a petrol station
3 on a motorway
4 in a library
5 visiting people in hospital
6 in your school

2 Look at the signs below and state the rules connected with them using *not allowed to* and *not supposed to*.

No right turn

Don't drop litter! £20 fine

Thank you for not smoking in this office.

It is illegal to travel without a ticket.

Please keep our city clean. Don't drop litter.

No parking between 08.00 and 18.30.

Please do not talk to the driver.

3 🔊 **Listen to this announcement.**

Note down:
where the announcement is taking place.
what two things are not allowed.

5 Reading

UNDERSTANDING BOYS

BOYS AS BABIES

The education of children starts as soon as they are born; girls wear pink and boys wear blue; boys play with guns and girls play with dolls. Boys are allowed to make more noise and cause more trouble, while girls are supposed to be more interested in talking to and understanding people. This kind of education prepares boys for power in the world but for little else.

BOYS UNDER PRESSURE

A boy is under pressure in many ways. He is supposed to be 'macho' -- good at sport, able to stand up for himself in fights and to suffer pain without crying. If he can't, he is a 'wimp' and often other boys will tease and bully him, especially at school. Yet probably only a very few boys can do all of these things. All boys are different -- they have different needs and talents, likes and dislikes. Some boys are good at cooking and writing poetry whereas others are good at football or maths.

Boys aren't just 'machos' and 'wimps'; there are swots as well as sports stars, conformists as well as rebels, shy boys as well as girl-chasers. If we can assure them that all these types are okay, it may help to reduce the bullying of those boys who are the least macho.

Glossary
'machos' and **'wimps'** tough people and weak people, usually applied to men or boys
swot a person who studies hard all the time

Before you read
1 Do you have any brothers or sisters? Did your parents bring you up differently from them? In what ways?
2 What sort of toys did you have as a child?
3 Can you remember any bullies at your school?
4 What do you think of men who cry?

Guess the meaning
under pressure   stand up for himself   suffer
tease   bully   conformist   rebel   reduce

COMPREHENSION
Read the article on the right and answer the questions.
1 How do parents often distinguish between baby boys and baby girls?
2 In what ways are boys supposed to be 'macho'?
3 What often happens to boys who are not macho?
4 How can we reduce bullying?

THINK ABOUT IT
1 What are girls supposed to be good at?
2 How does this influence the way girls plan their future?

WRITING
Linking devices: *both . . . and, as well as, neither . . . nor*

She likes **both** watching football **and** playing it.
She likes watching football **as well as** playing it.
Football is **neither** fun to play **nor** very exciting to watch.

Write sentences of your own, using each of the linking devices above.

VOCABULARY
'macho' is the opposite of *'wimp'*, and *rebel* is the opposite of *conformist*.

Use a dictionary to find the opposites of:
big   brave   extrovert   hard
hardworking   noisy   strong   tall

–6–
Grammar

Past simple and continuous

One evening last year Sue drove into a garage to get some petrol.
While she was paying for the petrol, a boy stole her wallet from the car.

Which tense is used in the first sentence above and which tenses in the second sentence?
Look at the Focus section below and notice how the tenses are used.

FOCUS

The past simple
This tense is used
- to talk about complete actions or events in the past. The tense is often linked to a time expression like *yesterday, last summer, in 1980*:
  One evening last year Sue drove into a garage to get some petrol.

The past continuous
This tense is used
- to talk about an activity which someone was in the middle of doing at a certain time in the past:
  What were you doing at six o'clock last night?
  I was watching the news on television.

- to talk about interrupted events in the past:
  While/When/she was paying for the petrol, a boy stole her wallet from her car.
  The position of *when* can be changed to give dramatic emphasis:
  She was paying for her petrol when suddenly a boy knocked her over and took her wallet.

- to describe background detail when telling a story:
  It was a warm summer's day. The sun was shining and the birds were singing.

What's the difference in meaning?

1 When she woke up, the telephone rang.
2 When she woke up, the telephone was ringing.

UNIT 6: Grammar

```
TRAVEL SCHEDULE - Thursday

7.30              Arrive at NBC studios.
7.45 - 9.00       Have breakfast with the producer
                  of Musical Box.
9.15              Leave the studio.
9.15 - 10.30      Drive to the concert hall in
                  Pasadena.
11.00 - 12.30     Interview jazz singer Dee Dee
                  Bridgewater.
1.00 - 1.45       Have lunch with Dee Dee's
                  manager.
2.00 - 5.00       Take photographs of
                  Dee Dee Bridgewater.
6.00              Leave the concert hall to
                  return to the motel.
7.30 - midnight   Attend a party in Hollywood.
12.30             Return to the motel.
```

PRACTICE

1 Sue Barnes is a young Scottish music journalist on her first visit to California. Look at the travel notes above for the last day of her visit. In pairs, ask and say what Sue did: 1 before lunch, 2 after lunch, 3 in the evening.

EXAMPLE
A: What did Sue do before lunch?
B: First she arrived and had breakfast at NBC studios. Then she …

2 In pairs, ask and say what Sue was doing at the following times:

| 1 8.00 | 3 12.00 | 5 3.00 p.m. |
| 2 10.00 | 4 1.30 p.m. | 6 9.00 p.m. |

EXAMPLE
1 A: What was Sue doing at eight o'clock?
  B: She was having breakfast at NBC studios.

3 Write the correct form of the verbs in brackets to complete and continue Sue's story. Use the past simple or the past continuous tense.

While Sue Barnes, a reporter for the New Musical Express, (travel) round the USA last year, she (have) an unpleasant experience. She had interviewed a jazz singer and had recorded the interview on a cassette which (be) on the front seat of her car together with other personal belongings.

She (drive) back to her motel after a party in Hollywood on her last night when she (realise) that she (run out) of petrol. She (stop) at an all-night garage just off the main highway. She (fill) the petrol tank, (take) 20 dollars from her wallet and (go) to the kiosk to pay. While she (pay), a boy suddenly (appear) from the shadows, (open) her car door and (take) her wallet, passport and return air ticket – and her cassette!

LISTENING

Listen to a friend of Sue's retelling the story at a party and note the details which he gets wrong.

WRITING

Write an account of an incident which has happened to you or someone you know. Say when and where the incident took place, who was involved and what they were doing at the time. Describe what happened, adding background details where necessary.

EXAMPLE
Last Saturday night I went with some friends to see the new Eddy Murphy film. We were queuing outside the cinema when suddenly a man came up . . .

CAPTAIN SENSIBLE

A ROOM OF MY OWN

photographed by Brian Moody

Captain Sensible, otherwise Raymond Burns, does not like his stage name. It is not clear exactly how he got it but it was something to do with wearing a peaked cap when he was touring France with his group, The Damned. 'We were fooling around on a plane journey when I announced: "This is your Captain speaking".'

That was eight years ago. Now twenty-eight, Captain Sensible is still living with his parents in a small terraced house in South London.

His room is a mess, knee-deep in clothes, shoes, magazines, paper and records. 'One of the music papers described me as one of the world's most disgusting slobs. It's true, I have to admit it.'

He was born in Balham and the family moved to the present house in Croydon in 1964 when he was six. 'When I left school, I swept factory floors and did a bit of gardening. We had a group, me, my younger brother and three friends. We thought we were the greatest. We weren't, we were rubbish. They stopped us halfway through our first number in a talent contest because we were making such a dreadful sound.'

Later, when Captain Sensible was working as a lavatory cleaner, a friend persuaded him to join his group, The Damned, as a bass player. He did, and that's how Captain Sensible started his career in the pop world.

After joining the group, he went to live in Brighton. He only stayed for eighteen months as he ended up living in a hovel. 'I'm not very good at doing the washing up and that. And when I was hungry, I used to open a tin and shove it on the cooker. I didn't like living like that so I thought, to hell with it, I'll go back and live with Mum and Dad.'

I asked him about his future in pop music. 'I don't think about it.' While we were talking, he puffed away at a cigarette. 'I smoke a lot. The world might end tomorrow, you know. We're just a speck in the universe, all of us.'

Glossary
stage name the name a performer uses
slob (coll) a rude, lazy and untidy person
Balham, Croydon suburbs of London
talent contest a competition for amateur performers

Since this interview was written, Cap... Sensible has married and no longer li... with his parents.

7

Topic

Living at home

Before you read

Look at the photograph and answer the questions.

1 What does the room tell you about its owner?
2 What do you think the man in the picture does for a living?
3 Would you like to have this room as your bedroom?

Words to learn

cap   mess   disgusting   admit   factory
rubbish   dreadful   cooker   universe

1 Read and find out:

1 how Raymond got the name 'Captain'.
2 what the name of his group is.
3 where he is living at the moment.
4 what he did when he left school.
5 what bad habits he has.

2 Write questions.

Write at least six questions which the interviewer asked Captain Sensible. Use the following question words: *How? Where? What? When? How long? Why?*

3 Read and think.

1 Why do you think he is called a 'disgusting slob'?
2 How do you think his parents feel about their son living at home?
3 What impression do you get of his character?

4 About you

1 Do you have a nickname? If so, how did you get it?
2 Are you a tidy person? How does your room look on a normal weekday morning?

VOCABULARY

1 Complete the list of adverbs below.

ADJECTIVE	ADVERB	ADJECTIVE	ADVERB
sensible	sensibly	hopeful	. . .
dreadful	dreadfully	wonderful	. . .
beautiful	. . .	helpful	. . .
awful	. . .	terrible	. . .

2 ■ Listen and note where the main stress falls on the adjective and adverb.

3 Which of the adjectives in Exercise 1 can follow *very*?

EXAMPLE: She is very sensible.

4 Which of the adverbs in Exercise 1 can be used instead of *very*?

EXAMPLE: It is dreadfully hot.

■ LISTENING

Listen to someone talking about an amusing incident. Note down the key points. Then listen again and note down any words or phrases about time. Use your notes to retell the story.

WRITING

Read the facts below about Captain Sensible, then write them in chronological order. Notice how the time connectors in italics link the facts.

1 *After joining* The Damned he went to live on his own in Brighton.
2 He joined the pop group The Damned *at the age of twenty* and changed his name from Raymond Burns to Captain Sensible *during* one of their tours abroad.
3 His family moved to Croydon *in 1964 when he was six.*
4 *Eventually,* he moved back home from Brighton to live with his parents.
5 *Now,* aged twenty-eight, Captain Sensible still lives with his parents.
6 Raymond Burns was born in Balham *in* 1958.
7 *At sixteen* he left school and worked as a sweeper in a factory *for a time.*

Now make notes about your own life or the life of someone in your family. Link these notes into a written paragraph using time connectors like those above.

8

Communication

Apologies

List as many ways of apologising as you can and then look at the picture and answer the questions.

1 Do you think the man in the picture is angry?
2 What is the girl saying?

📼 DIALOGUE

FATHER: What sort of time do you call this?
GIRL: I'm sorry.
FATHER: So you should be! It's two a.m!
GIRL: Oh Dad, do stop nagging. I'm over seventeen. It's up to me what time I come in.
FATHER: Not while you're living here, it isn't. Anyway, what on earth were you doing until two in the morning?
GIRL: We weren't doing anything. We were just talking.
FATHER: I was worried stiff about you.
GIRL: Honestly, Dad, I really am sorry, but you don't have to wait up for me, you know.
FATHER: O.K. I know you think I'm fussing and I'm sorry, but next time just let me know if you're going to be late, O.K? Give me a ring or something.
GIRL: Yes, O.K. I'll let you know next time. Sorry, Dad.
FATHER: That's O.K.

1 Listen and answer the questions.

1 Why is the girl's father angry?
2 What does the girl's father want her to do in future?
3 How often does the girl apologise? What does she say each time?
4 What three expressions does the father use in response to her apologies?

2 What do you understand by these idiomatic expressions?

1 What sort of a time do you call this?
2 So you should be.
3 It's up to me.
4 worried stiff
5 let me know
6 Give me a ring.

FOCUS

Apologies and responses

- Apologising:
  Sorry.
  I'm sorry.
  I'm terribly sorry.
  I'm awfully sorry.
  I really am sorry.

- Responding to apologies:
  That's O.K.
  That's all right.
  Don't worry about it.
  Never mind. It's nothing to worry about.
  It doesn't matter.

PRACTICE

1 Match the pictures 1 to 5 on the right with a suitable explanation from the list (a) to (e) below.

EXAMPLE
Picture 1 - b

a) There was a strike on the underground.
b) I wasn't looking where I was going.
c) I didn't realise it was so late.
d) I was only putting them back in the cupboard.
e) I thought it was mine.

Now, in pairs, act out each scene with an apology and explanation.

EXAMPLE
1 A: I'm sorry. I wasn't looking where I was going.
   B: That's O.K. There isn't much room in here.

2 In pairs, put the following situations in order from the least annoying to the most annoying.

1 A friend borrows your flippers to use on holiday and leaves them in the resort hotel.
2 A friend forgets to buy you some bread which you need for a party.
3 It is 3 a.m. The phone rings and it's a wrong number.
4 A friend spills black coffee over your new white jacket.

Now act out three of the situations in pairs.

EXAMPLE
A: I'm terribly sorry. I'm afraid I left your flippers in Ibiza.
B: Never mind. I can buy another pair.
A: Oh no, I'll get another pair for you.

LISTENING

Listen to an incident at a party and note:
1 what the woman did by accident.
2 how she apologised.
3 what the host said.
4 how the woman offered to make amends.
5 if her host accepted the offer.

Can you remember an incident when you had to apologise?

WRITING

Look at your notes from the Listening exercise and write the letter that the woman wrote to her host, Robert.
In your letter:
Thank Robert for the party and say how much you enjoyed it.
Apologise again for breaking the vase.
Make amends by asking if you can replace it.
Thank him again and say you hope to see him soon.

The following phrases may be useful:
I'm so sorry I . . . (past tense)
I'm terribly sorry about . . . -ing
I do apologise for . . . -ing
I'd like to . . .
I hope you'll let me . . .

—9—

Grammar

Used to and be used to

Sue says: 'I grew up on a farm, so we always had masses of meat and dairy products. We used to eat red meat nearly every day of the week, and we used to have butter and cream with everything. But a few years ago I became much more conscious of my diet. I don't eat red meat at all now, and very little butter or cream. I'm used to eating salads and vegetables instead, in fact I'm used to a much lighter diet.'

What's the difference in meaning?

1 I used to eat red meat.
2 I'm used to eating red meat.

FOCUS

'Used to' (past habit)

- *Used to* followed by an infinitive is always a past tense. It does not have a present form. The tense is used to show that something which regularly happened in the past, i.e. a past habit, no longer occurs now.
  (Past)   Years ago I used to eat a lot of red meat.
  (Present)   I don't eat red meat at all now.

'Be used to' (present custom)

- *To be used to* means *to be accustomed to* something. It can be followed by an *ing* form of the verb, or by a noun:
  I'm used to eating salads.
  I'm used to a lighter diet.

Find examples of the structures *used to* and *be used to* in the text about Sue at the top of the page.

PRACTICE

1 Match the sentences about Sue. Join the sentences with *but* and make statements about her life as a child compared with her life now, using *used to*.

EXAMPLE
Sue used to eat a lot of meat but now she is mainly vegetarian.

PAST HABITS
1 ate a lot of meat
2 had milk and cream with everything
3 went on holiday with her family
4 lived on a farm
5 drove a Fiat Uno

PRESENT HABITS
goes on holiday with friends
lives in a flat in Manchester
cycles everywhere
is mainly vegetarian
drinks tea and coffee without milk

2 Tell your partner about changes in your life concerning daily routine, family occasions, education and work using *used to*.

EXAMPLE
I used to eat a big breakfast before going to work, but I don't now.

UNIT 9: Grammar

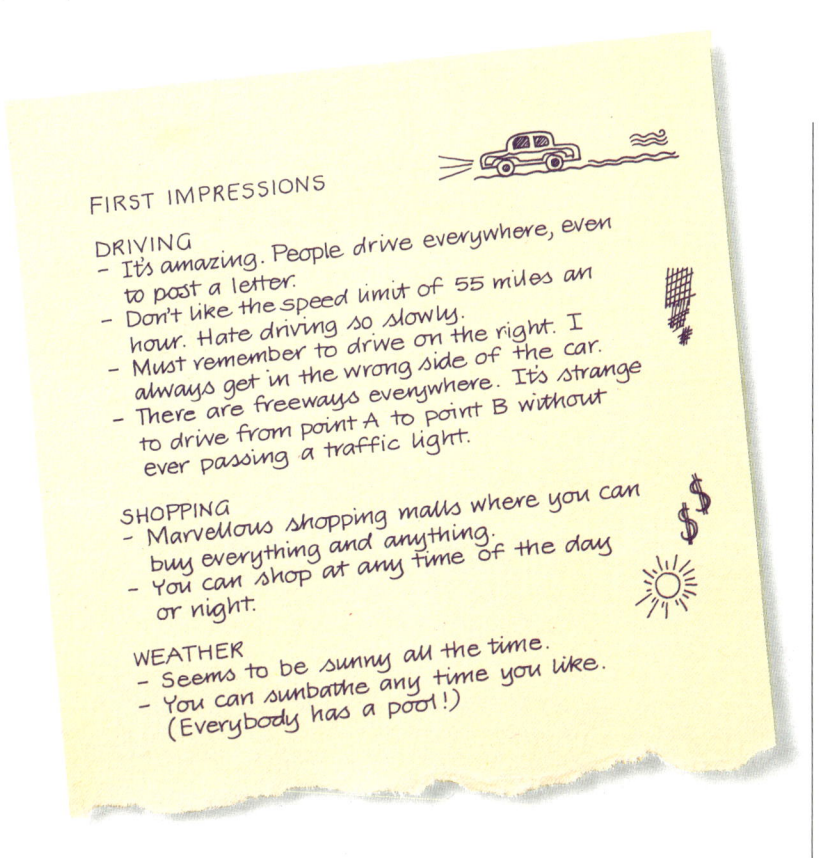

FIRST IMPRESSIONS

DRIVING
- It's amazing. People drive everywhere, even to post a letter.
- Don't like the speed limit of 55 miles an hour. Hate driving so slowly.
- Must remember to drive on the right. I always get in the wrong side of the car.
- There are freeways everywhere. It's strange to drive from point A to point B without ever passing a traffic light.

SHOPPING
- Marvellous shopping malls where you can buy everything and anything.
- You can shop at any time of the day or night.

WEATHER
- Seems to be sunny all the time.
- You can sunbathe any time you like. (Everybody has a pool!)

3 At the moment Sue has an assignment in California. She finds the lifestyle there very different from Britain. Imagine you are Sue. Use her notes above to say what you aren't used to in California.

EXAMPLE
I'm not used to driving everywhere.

4 Sue's brother, David, is in his first term at university. Read his account of being a student.

'At the moment it's a bit hard because I'm not used to living away from home. I have to do everything for myself, like cooking, washing and ironing. Mum used to do all that! Studying here is very different from school. We have to choose which lectures to go to and plan our own timetable. At school they used to tell you what to do and when to do it, but here you have more freedom. I'm not used to that so I often leave my essays to the last minute. Then I have to work right through the night, which is something I've never done before.'

5 Write as many sentences as you can about the things David is not used to doing.

EXAMPLE
He's not used to living away from home.

ACT IT OUT

In pairs, act out a conversation between Sue and a friend about how her brother is settling down at university.

Start like this:

FRIEND: How's your brother settling down at university?
SUE: O.K. but it's a bit hard for him because he's not used to living away from home.

LISTENING

Before you listen

Imagine you are spending some time in Britain. In groups, make a list of some of the features of the British way of life which you might find difficult or unusual. Here are some notes to start your list:
– speaking English all the time
– the noise and the traffic in London
– the unreliable English weather
– English money
– English food

Listen

Some young foreign students are studying in Britain. What features of British life aren't they used to? Are they the same as the ones you discussed?

WRITING

Imagine you are the last student in the Listening exercise. Write one paragraph of a letter to a penfriend describing the three aspects of British life which you are not used to. Link your sentences with:
Another thing is, . . . and
Also, . . .

EXAMPLE
When I first arrived, I wasn't used to the noise of the traffic and I couldn't sleep for three days, but it's all right now. Another thing was/is . . .

−10−
Reading

Cider with Rosie is a modern classic by Laurie Lee. It describes the time when he was growing up just after the First World War. Lee was one of a family of eight who lived in a cottage in the Cotswolds in what was then a remote part of the English countryside. The world which Laurie Lee describes has now vanished.

▶▶ CIDER WITH ROSIE ◀◀

With our mother, then, there were eight of us in that cottage, using rooms on its three large floors. There was the very big white attic where the girls used to sleep. On the floor below, Mother and Tony shared one bedroom; Jack, Harold and I had the other. But the house had been so often changed, since its building, that it was almost impossible to get to one's room without first passing through someone else's. So each night there was a procession of half-seen figures going sleepily to bed, until the last candle was blown out.

But most of the time when we were awake, while we were growing up, we spent in the kitchen. Until we married or ran away, it was the common room we all shared. In it, we lived and ate in the thick air of crowded family life; we didn't mind the little space; we trod on each other like birds in a nest, pushed past each other without unfriendliness, all talking at the same time or all silent. But we never, I think, felt overcrowded, because we were as separate as the notes of a piano.

That kitchen, showing the marks of our boots and our lives, was untidy, warm and low. Its muddle of furniture seemed never the same; it was moved around every day. Coal and sticks of beech wood crackled in a black fireplace and stove; towels hung to dry on the fireguard; the mantelpiece above the stove held an untidy collection of fine old china and potatoes of unusual shape. On the floor there were strips of muddy matting; the windows were crowded with plants in pots; the walls supported stopped clocks and picture postcards. There were six tables of different sizes; some armchairs with their insides bursting out; boxes, books and papers on every chair; a sofa for cats, a small organ for coats, and a piano for dust and photographs. And on the floor all round everything, the years had made shapeless piles of Mother's newspapers.

Glossary
the Cotswolds a hilly area in the west of England famous for its picturesque countryside and villages
beech a tall tree with dark green or copper-coloured leaves
organ a musical instrument, made of many pipes, played like a piano and often found in churches

UNIT 10: Reading

Before you read

1 Look at the illustration. What details make the house seem old-fashioned?
2 Write down as many words as you can which are connected with rooms, furniture and fittings.

Guess the meaning

attic   share   procession
candle   trod (tread)   crackle
mantelpiece   matting
bursting out   shapeless piles

COMPREHENSION

1 Answer the questions.

1 How many people lived in the cottage?
2 Where did the family spend most of their time?
3 What musical instruments were there in the kitchen?

2 Correct the statements.

EXAMPLE
1 Laurie Lee grew up in a small cottage.
   No, Laurie Lee grew up in a large cottage.

2 The girls slept in separate rooms.
3 The kitchen had a very high ceiling.
4 The kitchen had a fitted carpet.
5 There were six tables of the same size.
6 All the books were in a bookcase.
7 The newspapers were all in very neat piles.

THINK ABOUT IT

1 Do you think Laurie Lee came from a wealthy family?
2 Why do you think some of the family ran away?
3 What do you think Laurie Lee's mother was like?

ABOUT YOU

1 How big is your family?
2 What interesting things do your remember from your childhood?
3 Do any of your older relatives have interesting memories of how life used to be?

STYLE

1 Look at these similes from the text. They describe one thing by comparing it with another.

as separate as the notes of a piano   like birds in a nest

Complete the similes below.

as white as . . .   as strong as . . .   as tall as . . .
She/He sang like . . .   She/He swam like . . .   She/He ran like . . .

2 What do the following phrases tell you about life in the cottage?

a sofa for cats   a piano for dust   an organ for coats

TALKING POINT

What are the advantages and disadvantages of growing up in a large family?

VOCABULARY

Look at the following nouns from the text:

fireplace   fireguard

Link a word from the top line with a word from the bottom line to form a compound noun.

arm   house   table   candle   window   wash   book   dining
sill   basin   case   chair   work   room   cloth   stick

🔊 **Listen to the words and copy them, writing the main stess in capital letters. On which half of the noun does the stress usually fall?**

WRITING

Think of an interesting room and describe it.
PARAGRAPH 1:   Say which room you have chosen and where it is. Mention its size and its position in the house.
PARAGRAPH 2:   Describe what it looks like: the colours, the furniture and any ornaments and flowers.
PARAGRAPH 3:   Describe the atmosphere of the room and how you feel when you are in it.

EXAMPLE
The room I am going to describe is my grandmother's sitting room in her cottage in Wales. It's quite a large room on the ground floor.

The colours of the room are very warm. The wallpaper is . . . There are lots of . . .

There is a fire burning in the fireplace, even in summer, so the room is always warm and cosy. I love . . .

Self check 1

Units 1–10

1 Write the correct form of the verbs in brackets, using the present simple or present continuous tenses.

1 Could you sit down, please? I can't see what he (do).
   Could you sit down, please? I can't see what he's doing.

2 She (cycle) five miles to school and back every day.
3 The children (start) French at school next year.
4 He (not like) coffee with sugar.
5 I never (work) at the weekend.
6 They (travel) round the United States at the moment.
7 Ssh! I can't hear what she (say).
8 You (speak) Spanish as well as French?
9 I (try) to teach my brother to drive.
10 She (hate) working in the centre of the city.

2 Complete the boxes with the correct form of the verb.

Present	Past
buy	bought
go	
	won
	ran
take	
	gave
come	
tell	
	said
lose	

Present	Past
do	
make	
	saw
bring	
	spoke
read	
know	
	forgot
steal	
	found

3 Choose the correct verb tense and then rewrite the sentences.

1 While I *was having/had* breakfast this morning, my sister phoned from Mexico.
   While I was having breakfast this morning, my sister phoned from Mexico.

2 When I *was seeing/saw* his face, I *was realising/realised* my mistake.
3 It *was raining/rained* hard this morning when I *was waking/woke* up.
4 I *was writing/wrote* a letter to my Italian penfriend last night.
5 I *was taking/took* an umbrella because it *was raining/rained*.
6 It was a cold winter night. It *was snowing/snowed* hard and I *was wanting/wanted* to get back home quickly.

4 Write sentences choosing the correct form of *used to* and *be used to*.

1 (I'm not used to/I didn't use to) getting up early.
   I'm not used to getting up early.

2 (Are you used to/Did you use to) live near here?
3 (I'm used to/I used to) English food.
4 (Did you use to/Are you used to) wear glasses?
5 (I used to/I wasn't used to) doing my own washing.
6 (She's used to/She used to) living in a hot climate.
7 (She didn't use to/She isn't used to) eat any vegetables.
8 (He's used to/He used to) driving a sports car.

Self check 1

5 Complete the text by inserting one of the verb phrases below.

not allowed to   has to   have to
not supposed to   didn't have to
was allowed to

I've got a new job as a security guard and it's a big change. We . . (have to) . . clock in at 7.30 but in my last job we . . . start until eight o'clock. Also in my last job I . . . take an afternoon off every two weeks but here we don't get any half days. They're strict about smoking too but I think that's good. We're . . . smoke anywhere in the building. Anyone who wants to smoke . . . go outside. But they're not so strict about the lunch hour. We're . . . take more than an hour off but everyone does. Nobody seems to mind very much if you're a bit late back.

6 Write a sentence about each of the following:

1 a sport you enjoy doing
  I enjoy swimming.

2 two things you do every morning
3 what you are wearing at the moment
4 three things you did yesterday
5 what you were doing at nine o'clock last night
6 something you used to like doing when you were younger
7 something you weren't allowed to do at school
8 something that you're not supposed to do in your English class (but which you sometimes do).

7 Choose the best sentence or expression.

1 In a record store you want to buy the album of the Live Aid concert.

   a) I want the album of the Live Aid concert.
   b) Have you got the album of the Live Aid concert?
   c) Give me the Live Aid album.

2 You decide not to buy the new Simply Red compact disc.

   a) I think I'll leave it, thanks. It's not the one I want.
   b) I don't want it.
   c) I'm leaving it.

3 You knock someone's bag by accident while you are leaving the record store.

   a) Sorry!
   b) Never mind.
   c) I really am sorry. I'll get you another one.

8 Reorder the conversation.

Number the following lines in the correct order to make a conversation between a customer and a sales assistant in a stationery shop.

EXAMPLE
1 B Can I help you?

   A What about these then? They're Italian. They come in several pastel colours.
   B Can I help you?
   C Yes, we have. We've got some in red, green, yellow . . . or were you looking for a special colour?
   D O.K. Fine. Next please.
   E Yes, have you got any pencil holders?
   F Yes, they are nice but the colour's not quite right. I think I'll leave it.
   G Well, actually I'd like something pastel to match my room.

9 Agree or disagree with the following statements. Use *So do I* or *Nor do I* to agree, and *I do* or *I don't* to disagree.

1 I honestly think he's mad. (Agree)
  So do I.

2 I don't like people who smoke without asking permission. (Agree)
3 I don't think boxing is a proper sport. (Disagree)
4 I think there should be more women police. (Agree)
5 I think she's wasting her time at that school. (Disagree)
6 I don't think it's right to close the library early on Saturday. (Disagree)

10 What would you say in the following situations?

1 You are at the box office at the theatre. You would like to see the ballet 'Romeo and Juliet' tonight. Ask if they have any tickets left.

2 Your alarm clock didn't go off this morning so you missed the bus and arrived very late for class. Apologise and explain why you were late.

3 You ask to see a mug in a souvenir shop. When the assistant shows it to you, you realise you don't like the design. Decide not to buy it and thank the assistant.

4 Your friend breaks one of your glasses by accident and apologises. The glasses are not valuable. What do you say?

27

STUDY PROGRAMME

Classes take place daily from Monday to Friday from 9 a.m. until 12.30 p.m.

Afternoons are free for sightseeing or further study.

You will receive a detailed timetable when you arrive.

YOUR HOST FAMILY

Mr and Mrs Price,
36 Market Street,
Corsham,
Wiltshire

Telephone: 0249 88765

POLITE REMINDERS

Please remember that you are a guest in a family so:

- be punctual for all meals.
- always keep your room tidy.
- no smoking or alcoholic drinks in your room.
- always inform your host if you are going to be late back at night.

STUDY TRIPS

TRAVEL ARRANGEMENTS

Friday 20th June

Arrive London Heathrow 12.30.

Coach to Paddington Station.

Catch 15.30 train to Chippenham.

Arrive at 16.45.

Host family will meet you.

(Please write and confirm your travel arrangements with your English host family.)

Fluency 1

A study trip to Britain

You are going on a study trip to Britain. Use the information on this page to complete the tasks.

1 Telephone conversation

An English friend telephones you about the trip and wants to know:

who you are staying with.
if there are any children in the family and how old they are.
what the house is like.
what your study programme is.

2 Letter to your host

Write a short letter to your host and hostess, introducing yourself and confirming your travel arrangements. Say what you look like and say how much you are looking forward to staying with them.

3 A conversation

Act out a conversation with your host/hostess. The host/hostess asks about your trip and about your family back home. He/She is interested in your daily routine at home and wants to know what sort of food you like and what time you're used to eating.

4 An apology

You are at a disco and don't notice the time until after midnight. Telephone your host and apologise for phoning so late. Say where you are and how you are getting home. Say that you will try not to disturb the family when you come in.

5 A nasty incident

Just as you are leaving the disco, a fight breaks out and someone gets hurt. As you are a witness, the police ask you to go to the police station the next day. Act out the interview with the police officer. Tell the police officer what happened, and what you were doing at the time.

6 A postcard home

Write a postcard to your English teacher saying how you are enjoying your stay and if you are learning anything. Comment on the weather and say what you are doing in your free time.

Introducing Angie

Look at the pictures of Angie. What's she wearing and what do you think her job is?
Do you think she's well-paid?
How does she spend her free time?
Where do you think she lives?

Now read about Angie. Were you right?

29

−11−
Angie

A motorcycle courier

Most people hate traffic jams but not nineteen-year-old Angie Griffin. Angie is a motorcycle courier whose job involves delivering important packages and letters to different parts of London. She actually enjoys the day-to-day battle with the London traffic, especially the thrill of getting somewhere fast. She likes being a courier even though some people think it is not a very suitable job for a woman.

'I can't understand what they're talking about,' says Angie. 'The only trouble is they don't pay me enough! I'm going to ask for a rise next month.'

Angie was born and brought up in London. She lives with her mother in the rapidly developing dockland area of the East End.

'Everyone is moving here now. It's full of yuppies and BMWs. It'll be like Manhattan in a few years' time, full of skyscrapers. My mum says the cost of living is going up so much we won't be able to live here much longer.'

When Angie is not at work she is a bit of a fitness fanatic. She belongs to a health club and goes there regularly after work.

'I'd like to get a job connected with sport. I'm certainly not going to be a courier for ever. Sometimes I dream of being a sports photographer or a journalist. I often tell my mum: "One day, when I'm rich and famous, I'll buy you a house in the country." But all she really wants is to be able to stay where she is in the East End of London! I can't understand that. I want to get out and do something with my life.'

Glossary
yuppies (coll) young urban professional people with high incomes and fashionable lifestyles.
Manhattan the fashionable centre of New York City, famous for its skyscrapers

UNIT 11: Angie

Words to learn
courier   traffic jam   deliver   package
suitable   rise   brought (bring) up
develop   go up   fanatic

1 Read and answer.
1 What does Angie's job involve?
2 What does she like about it?
3 What is she going to do next month?
4 Where does she live?
5 What does she do in her spare time?
6 What sort of job does she dream of doing in the future?
7 What does she want to buy for her mother?
8 How is Angie different from her mother?

2 Read and think.
1 Why do some people think that Angie's job is not suitable for a woman?
2 What advantage do motorcyclists have in traffic?
3 Why is the cost of living going up in the dockland area?
4 Why do you think Angie doesn't want to be a courier for ever?

3 About you
1 When and where are the worst traffic jams in your city or in a city near you?
2 Are there any rapidly developing areas near you? Name some.

VOCABULARY

Many names for jobs and occupations end in the suffixes *er*, *or*, or *ist*, e.g: *photographer, actor, journalist*.

1 Complete the following with the correct suffix *er*, *or*, or *ist* to make names of jobs and occupations. Use your dictionary to help you. Add similar words of your own.

EXAMPLE: painter

paint-	scient-	pharmac-
telephon-	inspect-	danc-
plumb-	butch-	physic-
reception-	survey-	wait-
solicit-	typ-	jewell-
doct-	carpent-	dent-

2 🖭 Now listen and copy the words, writing the stressed syllable in capital letters.

EXAMPLE
PAINTer   teLEPHonist

TALKING POINT

Give examples of jobs which some people think may be unsuitable for men or women. Say what *you* think and discuss your reasons in groups. The following expressions may be useful:

What about a butcher, for example?
Why shouldn't a woman be a butcher?

Take a butcher, for example.
There's absolutely no reason why a butcher can't be a woman.

ABOUT BRITAIN

The development of London's Docklands

The dockland area in the East End of London used to be, as the name suggests, a busy port. Ships from all over the world docked and unloaded cargo there. After the 1960s the London docks went into decline. The docks were too small to handle the large modern container ships and the loading and unloading facilities were out of date.

However, since the 1980s, a new dockland has developed in the East End, with modern offices and homes, marinas, a new railway system and even a small airport. The old EastEnders say that rich newcomers are pushing up house prices and the cost of living. Their message is: 'Yuppies — Go back where you came from.'

🖭 LISTENING

Listen to Doris, a fruit and vegetable stall holder in Docklands, talking about the changes she sees around her.

Note down complaints she makes.

Grammar

Future tenses: *going to* and *will*

What's the difference in meaning?

1 I'm going to phone him in the morning.
2 I'll phone him in the morning.

Look back at the text about Angie in Unit 11 and notice the other ways in which *going to* and *will/won't* are used. Check the Focus section below to see if you know the different uses of the two tenses.

FOCUS

'Going to'

This tense is used

- to talk about planned decisions and intentions:
  I'm going to ask for a rise next month.
- to talk about future arrangements:
  He's going to stay with us for a week.
- to make predictions about the immediate future when there is some evidence to show what is going to happen:
  Look at those black clouds. It's going to rain in a minute.

'Will'

This tense is used

- to make predictions about the future:
  The Docklands will be like Manhattan in a few years' time.
  We won't be able to live here much longer.
- to make statements of fact about the future:
  Steve will be thirty next birthday.
- to make a decision at the moment of speaking:
  I'll tell him tonight.
- to make a promise or offer:
  I'll post those letters for you.
- with clauses of condition and time:
  If/When I'm rich, I'll buy you a house in the country.

PRACTICE

1 In pairs, practise the following dialogue several times, choosing different words and phrases each time.

A: What are you going to do tomorrow?
B: We're going to spend the day
   in the country.
   in the mountains.
   by the lake.
   on the coast.
A: Well, they say it's going to
   rain.
   be cold.
   freeze.
   be very windy.
   snow.
   be lovely and sunny.
B: In that case I'll take my
   skis.
   swimming things.
   skates.
   anorak.
   shorts.
   thick jacket.
   raincoat.

2 Find out:

1 what your friends are going to do this weekend.
2 what your teacher is going to do immediately after this lesson.
3 if anyone is going to change their schools or move home in the near future.
4 the weather forecast for tomorrow. Is it going to be warm and sunny or wet and cold?

3 Match the words and phrases in the two columns below to talk about your arrangements for the coming weekend.

EXAMPLE
1 I'm going to write some letters.

1 write	my room
2 phone	some letters
3 do	my bike
4 repair	a cake
5 buy	my girl/boyfriend
6 take back	last week's homework
7 tidy	a new pair of jeans
8 make	my library books

Now add some plans of your own.

4 Exchange the lists above with your partner. Imagine that it is now Monday morning. Admit that you forgot to do each activity and decide when you intend to do it, using *will*.

EXAMPLE
A: Did you write any letters?
B: No, I forgot but I'll write some tomorrow morning/afternoon/evening.

LISTENING

1 Listen to Angie talking to a friend of hers, Colin.

Note down:
why Angie phones Colin.
why Colin can't come.
what he suggests.
what he offers to do.

2 Listen again and complete the dialogue with the correct form of *going to, will* or the present continuous.

ANGIE: Colin? It's Angie.
COLIN: Oh, hi Angie! How are things?
ANGIE: O.K, thanks. Listen, (1) . . . anything on Saturday?
COLIN: Saturday? I'm not sure. Why?
ANGIE: Well, it's the international athletics meeting at Crystal Palace. I've got two tickets. I think it (2) . . . good. Do you want to come?
COLIN: It sounds fun. (3) . . . my diary. Hang on.
ANGIE: O.K.
COLIN: Let's see. Oh, that's a pity!
ANGIE: What's wrong?
COLIN: (4) . . . in a college football match that afternoon, I'm afraid.
ANGIE: That's a shame! Who else can I ask?
COLIN: You could ask Mike. He's quite keen on athletics.
ANGIE: Yes, O.K. What's his number?
COLIN: I can't remember. But I know he's (5) . . . at college this afternoon. (6) . . . him to phone you.
ANGIE: Fine. I (7) . . . home about nine.
COLIN: O.K.
ANGIE: Thanks. Look, I'd better go. I (8) . . . late for work if I'm not careful. Bye for now!
COLIN: Bye Angie!

Practise reading your completed dialogue with your partner.

WRITING

Write the note to Mike which Colin leaves on the college notice board to tell him about Angie's phone call.

Start like this:

Dear Mike,
Sorry I missed you but I've got a message from Angie. She's got . . . I can't go myself because . . . so she wondered if you . . .

33

—13—
Communication

Requests

Look at the photograph below and answer the questions.

1 What is the receptionist giving Angie?
2 What is Angie going to do?
3 What do you think the receptionist is saying to Angie?

🖥 DIALOGUE

RECEPTIONIST: Could you take this to the Computer Centre in Allington Street, please?
ANGIE: Where's that?
RECEPTIONIST: It's off Buckingham Palace Road.
ANGIE: Right. That'll be £12.50 . . . Thanks. That's £2.50 change.
RECEPTIONIST: Could I have a receipt?
ANGIE: Yes, sure.
RECEPTIONIST: Thank you. And do you think you could hurry? It is rather urgent.
ANGIE: Yes, I'll do my best, but it is the rush hour.
RECEPTIONIST: By the way, would you mind asking them to call me as soon as they get it?
ANGIE: O.K.
RECEPTIONIST: Thanks very much.

Listen and answer the questions.

1 What does the receptionist want Angie to do?
2 How much does she give Angie?
3 What does she ask Angie for?
4 What time of day do you think it is?
5 How many requests are there in the dialogue?

FOCUS

Polite requests

- Asking for things:
  Could I have a receipt?
  Do you think I could have a receipt?

- Asking people to do things:
  Could you take this to the Computer Centre, please?
  Do you think you could hurry?
  Would you mind asking them to call me?

- Agreeing to do things:
  O.K.
  Yes, sure.
  Yes, certainly.
  Yes, of course.
  Yes, I'll do that.

Note
1 *Would you mind . . .,* is more formal.
2 *Please* is not always necessary if a polite intonation is used.

UNIT 13: Communication

ACT IT OUT

You want a taxi to take you to different places in London. Act out a conversation with the taxi driver. Use the dialogue with Angie and the information below to help you. Include different forms of polite requests in your conversation.

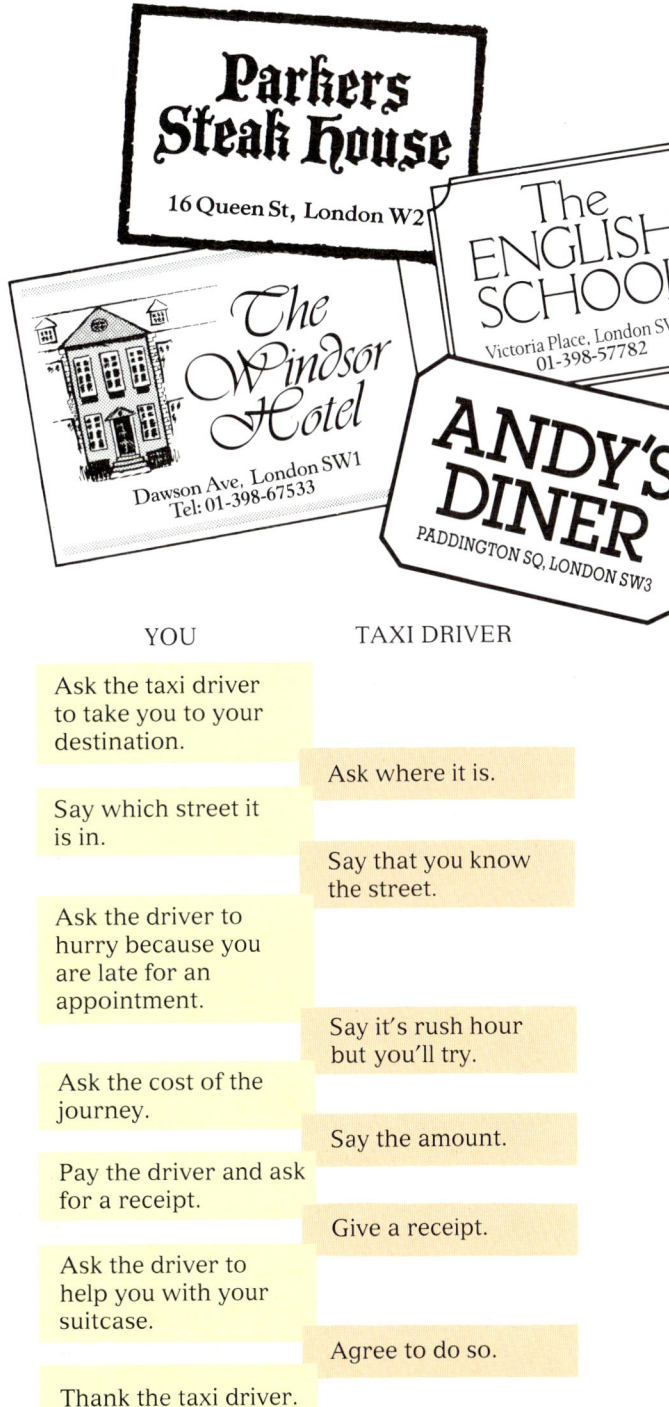

Parkers Steak house
16 Queen St, London W2

The Windsor Hotel
Dawson Ave, London SW1
Tel: 01-398-67533

The ENGLISH SCHOOL
Victoria Place, London SW1
01-398-57782

ANDY'S DINER
PADDINGTON SQ, LONDON SW3

PRACTICE

1 Write a suitable caption for each of the pictures above, using a request each time.

2 You are staying as a paying guest with a British family. In pairs, decide what you would say in the following situations.

1 You would like an extra pillow on your bed.
2 You ask a ten-year-old in the family to post your letters.
3 You don't like coffee. Ask for tea without milk for breakfast.
4 You forget your keys. When you arrive home the house is empty. You go next door and ask to use the telephone to phone your host at work.
5 You would like your teacher to sign an application form for a student travel card.

WRITING

You are ill in bed with flu. Write a note to your English teacher. Explain that you can't come to class for a few days. Say you would like to do some homework while you are away. Ask your teacher to tell a friend in your class what you should do. Say you are also enclosing an application form for a student travel card and ask your teacher to sign it. Say when you hope to be back in class.

LISTENING
Before you listen

What do the following words have in common?
street   square   gardens
lane   avenue   road

Listen

A client calls a courier office with a request. Listen and note the name and address of the client, the delivery address and the cost.

YOU	TAXI DRIVER
Ask the taxi driver to take you to your destination.	
	Ask where it is.
Say which street it is in.	
	Say that you know the street.
Ask the driver to hurry because you are late for an appointment.	
	Say it's rush hour but you'll try.
Ask the cost of the journey.	
	Say the amount.
Pay the driver and ask for a receipt.	
	Give a receipt.
Ask the driver to help you with your suitcase.	
	Agree to do so.
Thank the taxi driver.	

Cynthia could never fully understand . . .

. . . the joys of riding . . .

—14—

Grammar

Ability and possibility: can, could and be able to

FOCUS

'Can'/'could'

These are used

- to talk about ability:
  She can sing well but she can't read music.
  When I was young, I could dance quite well but I'm hopeless now.

- to talk about possibility:
  I can come on Monday.
  She couldn't go to the party because she was ill.

- with certain verbs that do not usually occur in the present continuous tense, e.g. *remember, understand, smell, hear, feel, taste, see*:
  I can/could smell something burning.
  I can't understand anything.

'Be able to'

This is used

- to give emphasis to a statement of ability or possibility:
  After her illness she wasn't able to walk for a year.
  We won't be able to live here much longer.
  The use of *couldn't* and *can't* in these two examples would be correct but less forceful.

- to express the meaning of *manage to* or *succeed in* concerning one specific occasion:
  Although the sea was rough, they were able to (= managed to) swim to the shore.
  Luckily they heard the alarm and were able to escape.
  Here the use of *could* would not be correct.

- to replace the infinitive and the 'missing' tenses (e.g. the present perfect) of *can* and *could*:
  I'd love to be able to sing well.
  She hasn't been able to get tickets for the concert.

- on formal occasions (especially when written):
  I am afraid we are unable to offer you a refund on your ticket.

Note

1 *Couldn't* (but not *could*) is possible in all situations.
2 The negative of *able to* is *not able to* or *unable to*.

PRACTICE

1 In pairs, use the phrases below to make and respond to requests.

EXAMPLE
A: Could you help me with my project some time this week?
B: I'm afraid I can't this week but I might be able to help you next week.

REQUEST	TIME	ALTERNATIVE
help me with my project	some time this week	next week
come to lunch	on Tuesday	on Wednesday
help me buy a new suit	next week	the week after
look at my computer	this weekend	next weekend
translate a letter	this evening	tomorrow evening

2 Complete the sentences with *can*, *could* or *be able to*. Sometimes more than one answer is possible.

1. Oh dear, I (not) . . . remember her address.
2. I used to . . . wiggle my ears but I can't any more.
3. Where are the keys? I (not) . . . find them last night.
4. She's moved to York so she will . . . see her parents more often.
5. The theatre seats were awful. We (not) . . . see the stage.
6. The show is very popular but luckily I . . . get two seats for Saturday.
7. My car broke down and I haven't . . . drive it for a week.
8. The exam was easy. I . . . do all the questions.
9. It's nice . . . sleep late on Sundays.
10. My sister (not) . . . swim until she was eleven.
11. After the accident he (not) . . . smell or taste anything.
12. I lost all my money but fortunately I . . . borrow some from friends.

ACT IT OUT

Act out the following situation in pairs. Use the grammar you learnt in Unit 12 as well as in this unit.

A
You have decided you are going to spend a year abroad. You have some savings in the bank but you would like to borrow £500 from your parents. Try and persuade your parents to lend you the money. Decide how and when you intend to pay them back.

B
Your daughter/son wants to borrow £500 so she/he can spend a year abroad. You are not too keen on the idea. You want to know where she/he is going, where she/he is going to live and what she/he is going to do. You also want to know how and when you will get your money back.

WRITING

Write a letter inviting some English-speaking guests to the theatre.

PARAGRAPH 1
Explain that you were able to get tickets for a popular show. Say which show and when the performance is.

PARAGRAPH 2
Apologise and explain that you won't be able to meet them at their hotel and ask them to meet you at the theatre instead.

PARAGRAPH 3
Ask them to telephone you to say if they can come or not. Say where you will be and when they can contact you.

(Your address)
(the date)

Dear . . .,
After our conversation last week, I telephoned the theatre and luckily I . . . tickets for . . . on . . . and I hope you . . .

I'm afraid I won't . . . because . . . so . . .
Could you . . . I'll be . . .
With best wishes,

Yours sincerely,

. . . until she was finally able to control her horse.

HIDDEN LONDON

WONDERFUL TOURS LTD

TOUR 3

Whole day and evening
£45 (inc. lunch and entrances)
Departs: *Saturday and Sunday*
- *Pick-up service from main hotels*
- *Optional evening activities include night clubbing or a mediaeval banquet.*

This unforgettable whole day and evening tour includes places which are off the traditional tourist route. We will take you where real Londoners go and we guarantee you will have the experience of a lifetime.

CAMDEN LOCK MARKET

We will start our tour at the busy and fashionable Camden Lock Market, which is famous for its street-wise fashion and which is rapidly becoming *the* place to be seen in. There are over two hundred stalls selling everything from homemade fudge to ethnic jewellery. You will have time to browse among the stalls and perhaps find that special present to take home before you embark on......

JASON'S RIVERBOAT

At Camden Lock you will find one of Jason's Riverboats waiting to take you on a gentle cruise along Regent's Canal, through the beautiful surroundings of Regent's Park and London Zoo. A delicious lunch will be served on board.

SOUTH BANK

After the boat trip, we rejoin our coach and make our way across London to the South Bank, a huge modern complex of theatres, concert halls and art galleries, situated on the South Bank of the River Thames. From there, you will get a spectacular view of Westminster and the Houses of Parliament across the river.

CHELSEA, KING'S ROAD, AND 'BOY' BOUTIQUE

Our route then takes us round the Embankment to Chelsea and the King's Road. The highlight will be a visit to 'Boy', the original punk shop in the King's Road, which many people think is the real heart of London. If you like people-watching, you'll love the King's Road.

Freshen-up time
There is now a three-hour break for you to change and freshen up back at your hotel.

NIGHT CLUB OR MEDIAEVAL BANQUET?

An evening choice
We will pick you up again at 9.00 p.m at your hotel for the evening entertainment.

For the young at heart we have a special Fish and Chip Supper at The Seashell, Lisson Grove. This restaurant is universally recognised as serving the best fish and chips in the world. After supper we proceed to The Wag Club, London's trendiest club.

For the historically minded we have arranged a Mediaeval banquet where you can wine and dine with King Henry VIII and his many wives. This magnificent five-course feast is accompanied by music and cabaret. You can even watch the beheading of Anne Boleyn!
Book now for a truly unforgettable day.

PICK UP TIMES:

Tara Hotel	8.50 a.m.
Russell Square Hotel	9.00 a.m.
London International	9.05 a.m.
Strand Palace Hotel	9.15 a.m.
Cumberland Hotel	9.45 a.m.
Coburg Hotel	10.00 a.m.

Reading

Before you read

1 Can you name any famous places in London?
2 Which places would you like to visit?
3 Are there interesting places in your city which tourists rarely visit?

Guess the meaning

street-wise   browse   ethnic   embark
on board   complex   spectacular   banquet

COMPREHENSION

1 Read the brochure on the left and identify each of the photographs.

EXAMPLE
1 Camden Lock Market

2 In pairs, take it in turns to be a tourist who is interested in going on this tour. Ask and answer questions to find out:

1 what sort of tour it is.
2 how much it costs.
3 if you can go on Sundays.
4 if lunch is included.
5 if the tour includes a visit to Madame Tussaud's.
6 what you can do in the evening.
7 what time the coach leaves the Russell Square Hotel in the morning.

EXAMPLE
A: What sort of tour is it?
B: It's a whole day and evening tour of places in London which are off the traditional tourist route.

TALKING POINT

Discuss:

which part of the tour sounds the most boring and which the most interesting.
the advantages and disadvantages of going on a guided tour.

VOCABULARY

The prefix *un* can be used in front of many words to produce opposite meanings:

forgettable/unforgettable   happy/unhappy

Which of the following adjectives can be preceded by the prefix *un*?

tidy   usual   bad   helpful   interesting
nice   fortunate   necessary   popular
beautiful   kind

What are the opposites of the other words?

WRITING

Before you write

In pairs or groups, plan an unusual tour of a town or city. Plan where your group can have refreshments, lunch and dinner and how long the tour will last.

Write a description

Write a description of your tour, explaining why the places are famous or interesting. Link your ideas with a relative pronoun: *which, who* or *where*. Use the model below to help you.

TOUR OF . . . CITY

We will start our tour outside . . ., which is . . . From there we will go to . . ., which is/where you can . . .

After this, you will visit the palace/tomb/house of . . ., who was . . .

Finally, we will take a ride on the . . .

39

Grammar

First conditional and time clauses

Speech bubbles in illustrations:
- If it starts to rain, we'll play inside.
- If you bend your knees more, you'll keep your balance better.
- If you're late again, you won't be in the team!

Look at the pictures and answer the questions.

1 What will they do if it rains?

2 What will happen if she bends her knees more?

3 What will happen if he's late again?

In which sentence is the speaker doing the following:

giving advice?
talking about a possible future event?
giving a warning?

Which verb tense is used in the *if* clause and which verb tense in the main clause?

FOCUS

The first conditional: 'if' clauses + future

This structure is used
- to describe a possible future event and its consequences:
  If it starts to rain, we'll play inside.
- to give advice:
  If you bend your knees, you'll keep your balance better.
- to warn or threaten:
  If you're late again, you won't be in the team!

Time clauses with 'when' and 'as soon as'

- In time clauses, *as soon as* means *immediately,* but *when* is not so definite:
  I'll phone you as soon as I get home. (immediately)
  I'll phone you when I get home. (not so definite)

Points to note
- In certain cases, *will/won't* can be replaced by *going to*:
  If you're not home by six, I'm going to eat without you.
- *Unless* can replace *if . . . not* to add emphasis.
  If you don't go now, you'll miss the train.
  Unless you go now, you'll miss the train.
- The future tense is used in the main clause, but not in first conditional or time clauses.
- *Will/won't* can be replaced by certain modals, e.g. *may, can.*
  If it rains, we may go to the cinema.

What's the difference in meaning?

1 If I see Jan, I'll tell her about the match.
2 When I see Jan, I'll tell her about the match.

UNIT 16: Grammar

PRACTICE

1 Rewrite the sentences making the *if* clause negative. Make any necessary changes to the main clause to keep the same meaning.

EXAMPLE
1 If you work hard, you'll pass your exams.
 If you don't work hard, you won't pass your exams.

2 If you go to the market early, you'll get some fresh fish.
3 If you hurry, you'll catch the bus.
4 If I sell my car, I'll be able to afford a holiday.
5 If it's sunny, we'll go to the beach.
6 If I get a residence permit, I'll be able to stay in the USA.

2 Look at the sentences in Exercise 1 again. Rewrite them using *unless*.

EXAMPLE
You won't pass your exams unless you work hard.

3 Reply to the questions on the left choosing from the list on the right. Start with *I'll/We'll . . . as soon as . . .*

EXAMPLE
1 When are we going to eat?
b) We'll eat as soon as John gets back.

1 When are we going to eat?
2 When are you going to do your homework?
3 Aren't you going to leave soon?
4 When can you lend me that book?
5 When are you going to come and visit us?
6 When are you going to finish that report?

a) I finish reading it.
b) John gets back.
c) I get a free weekend.
d) this programme finishes.
e) I get my typewriter back.
f) the babysitter arrives.

4 Complete the conversation between Angie and her mother by writing the correct form of the verb in brackets.

MOTHER: I'm off to work now. What time will you be back?
ANGIE: About six. But I (ring) you if there (be) any problems.
MOTHER: Well, if you (be) back before me, you (have to) get something for supper.
ANGIE: O.K, I (decide) on something when I (get) to the supermarket.
MOTHER: If I (pass) a greengrocer's, I (buy) some strawberries.
ANGIE: Great!
MOTHER: Is Colin coming round tonight?
ANGIE: He didn't say but if he (get in touch), I (invite) him to supper.
MOTHER: Look at the time. I (miss) the bus unless I (go) now.
ANGIE: O.K. Bye. I (see) you when I (get) home.

5 In pairs or groups, complete these 'tips and hints'.

EXAMPLE
1 Your T-shirts won't shrink if . . .
 Your T-shirts won't shrink if you dry them naturally.

2 You'll get a smoother shave if . . .
3 If . . ., you'll tan more quickly.
4 If . . ., your skin may go dry.
5 Your roses will last longer if . . .
6 Your house plants will die unless . . .
7 Your car won't use so much petrol if . . .

6 Discuss your advice with your partner and the rest of the class. In pairs, write down three useful tips that you know.

LISTENING
Before you listen

Identify the following parts of the body:

back   head   arms   feet
fist   shoulder   mouth   nose

Listen

Listen to an interview with a trainer who gives advice on how to run properly. What advice does he give about the correct position of your body, your back, your head and your arms, and what does he advise about breathing?

WRITING

Write a short list of Dos and Don'ts for running, or another sport you know well, and give explanations for your advice.

EXAMPLE
DO
Wear comfortable shoes.
If you don't, you'll get blisters.

'The important thing in the Olympic Games is not winning but taking part.'

Baron de Coubertin.

THE OLYMPIC GAMES

When the next Olympic Games begin, satellites will carry T.V. pictures of the opening ceremony to millions of people thousands of miles away. From their armchairs these people will be able to see their country's athletes competing in events and maybe winning a bronze, silver or even gold medal.

When we consider the size, the spectacle and the commercialism of the modern Olympic Games, it is difficult to remember that they started in Olympia in Greece in 776 BC with only one race, a sprint, for which the prize for the winner was an olive wreath.

The idea of an international Olympic Games was conceived by a Frenchman, Baron Pierre de Coubertin and, appropriately, the first modern Olympic Games opened in Athens in 1896. Nowadays, major cities compete to host the Olympic Games, not just for the honour the Games bring, but for the vast amount of profit a host country can make.

The games have also become politically important. They can now be seen by nearly every country in the world and are therefore an ideal platform for political statements. When Soviet troops invaded Afghanistan in 1980, many countries in the West, including Britain and the United States, boycotted the Moscow Games. In 1984 some countries decided not to send teams to the Los Angeles Games because they felt there was not enough security and that they were too commercial.

In circumstances like these, the Olympic ideal and spirit comes into question. And for athletes there is less value in winning a gold medal if the best of the world's athletes are not competing. The question is – how much longer will the Games survive if nations continue to use them as a political platform?

17

Topic

Sport

Before you read

1 Which country started the Olympic Games?
2 Which country was host to the last Olympic Games?
3 Name an Olympic gold medal winner in the last Olympics.
4 Apart from gold, what other medals can athletes win?
5 Why did some countries boycott the 1980 Olympics?
6 Where are the next Games going to be held?

Words to learn

compete   vast   profit
commercial   political
ideal (adj)   invade
boycott   security

1 Read the article on the left and describe:

1 the main differences between the ancient and modern Olympic Games.
2 how certain nations have used the Olympics as a political platform.

2 Read and think.

1 Why was it appropriate that the Greeks should hold the first modern Olympics?
2 How can countries make a commercial profit from holding the Games?

3 About you

1 Have you ever been to the Olympic Games or watched them on TV?
2 Which events do you prefer?
3 What other sports do you enjoy watching or taking part in?

VOCABULARY

1 Look at the words below and find two water sports, two team sports, two winter sports, three indoor sports and two motor sports.

skiing   football   scrambling   ice skating   volleyball
boxing   swimming   windsurfing   motor racing
table tennis   gymnastics

2 Match the sporting event with the location.

EXAMPLE: ski slope

A: ski   swimming   athletics   boxing   skating   tennis
     golf   football

B: course   pitch   court   track   ring   rink   pool   slope

🔲 LISTENING

Listen to these commentaries and note which sports are taking place.

TALKING POINT

1 Why do athletes from the Soviet Union, the United States and East Germany usually win so many medals in the Olympic Games?
2 What do you think might be the disadvantages of holding the Olympic Games in your city or a city near you?

WRITING

Imagine your country has been chosen to host the next Olympic Games. You are worried about this decision and want to know how the city is going to raise the money to provide all the necessary extra facilities. Write a letter to a newspaper. Join your ideas with *not only . . . but also . . .* and *as well as.*

EXAMPLE

Dear Sir,

It has recently been announced that the next Olympics are going to be held in . . . .

As a resident of . . . I am very worried about this decision. If we hold the Games here, we will not only have to build a new . . . but also . . . several new . . . for the . . . .

The amount of extra traffic will be enormous and, as well as building . . ., they will also have to improve . . . .

What I would like to know is, how . . .?

Yours faithfully,

−18−

Communication

Checking information

DIALOGUE

Angie is talking to Carl, a neighbour.

ANGIE: Hi, Carl! What are you doing here? Aren't you supposed to be at school?
CARL: No, we've got the afternoon off. I wanted to go swimming at the sports centre but the pool's closed all this week.
ANGIE: Isn't there a pool in Lansbury Park?
CARL: Yes, but it's no good. It's too shallow and anyway all the kids go there.
ANGIE: What about the Oasis at Mile End? The 49 bus goes there, doesn't it?
CARL: Yes, but it takes so long.
ANGIE: Come on, lazy bones! I'll take you on the bike. Grab this helmet and jump on!

Listen and answer the questions.

1 Why isn't Carl at school?
2 Why can't he go swimming at the sports centre?
3 Why doesn't he want to go to the pool at Lansbury Park?
4 Why doesn't Carl want to go to the pool at Mile End by bus?
5 What does Angie offer to do?

FOCUS

Checking information

- Checking information:
  Isn't there a pool in Lansbury Park? (negative question)
  The 49 bus goes there, doesn't it? (tag question)

- Checking information with surprise:
  Aren't you supposed to be at school? (negative question)

PRACTICE

1 Rephrase each question in the Focus section using either a negative question or a tag question.

EXAMPLE
There's a pool in Lansbury Park, isn't there?

2 Write some facts about your partner which you are fairly sure about. Then check the facts using a tag question.

EXAMPLE
Notes:
Janine – is French
 – lives outside Paris
 – works in a bank

Questions:
You're French, aren't you?
You live outside Paris, don't you?

Check the facts again, using a negative question each time.

EXAMPLE
Aren't you French?

3 Indicate surprise in these holiday situations. Use a negative question each time.

EXAMPLE
1 It's 8.30 a.m. on a sunny morning and your friend is still in bed.
Aren't you going to get up?

2 At supper your friend leaves half a plate of chips on the plate.
3 In the morning in the bathroom your friend looks pale and is holding a packet of aspirin.
4 In the sea your friend puts on a pair of inflatable plastic arm bands.
5 At the bank your friend says: 'Where on earth is my passport?'
6 In a beach café you think you recognise an old school friend.

UNIT 18: Communication

WHEN IS A QUESTION NOT A QUESTION?

The answer to this could be: 'When it's a greeting'. Take 'How do you do?', for example. Although this ends in a question mark, it is not a question but a greeting. The correct response is to repeat the same 'question': 'How do you do?'

And again, if a friend stops you in the street and asks: 'How are you?', remember that this is not a true question. It would be extremely inappropriate to give a long description of your state of health. A simple 'Fine, thanks.' is all they wish to hear, even though you may be wrapped in bandages as you speak.

If someone says at table: 'Could you pass the milk?', they will be very surprised if you answer: 'Yes, I could.' This is not a question but a request. Likewise, 'Couldn't you go and fetch them, James?' sounds like a harmless question but is in fact a direct order to James.

How are you?
Fine, thanks!

LISTENING

1 Listen to two people who meet in the street.

1 What are their names?
2 What nationality is the man?
3 When did they first meet?
4 Why did he have to leave so quickly?
5 How does the man end the conversation in the street?

2 Listen again and copy down all the questions you heard.

ACT IT OUT

You meet someone in the street whom you think you saw at a party last week. You are fairly sure you remember his/her name. In pairs, act out a conversation. Mention the party and say how much you enjoyed it. Suggest the person comes and has a drink.

Start like this:

YOU: Hello! Didn't we meet at . . .
HE/SHE: Yes, that's right.
YOU: You're . . ., aren't you?

READING

Before you read
How do you answer the questions, *How do you do?* and *How are you?*

Read the text above and answer the questions.

1 How many different examples of questions which are not really questions are mentioned in the text?
2 List all the 'questions' and say what other meaning they have.

EXAMPLE
How do you do? = a greeting

WRITING

Write a paragraph about why you think English is an easy or difficult language to learn. You may like to mention the grammar, the vocabulary, the pronunciation and intonation, the spelling, the idioms or any other aspect which interests you.

Start like this:

I think English is quite a . . . language to learn. For example, . . . Another thing is . . . Also, . . . And finally, . . .

—19—

Grammar

In case

Here. Take this road map in case you get lost.

spare can of petrol
red triangle
road m[ap]
spare wheel
First Aid Kit

FOCUS
'In case'

- This structure is used to give the reason for doing something:
  Take this road map in case you get lost.
  The *in case* clause gives the reason for the main clause, i.e. the reason for taking a map.

Points to note

- *In case* cannot be followed by *will* or *going to*. The present tense is used to talk about the future in an *in case* clause:
  You need some coins in case you have to phone.
  Take some coins in case you need to phone.
  I'll take some coins in case I need to phone.

- *In case* can also be used to explain why someone did something in the past:
  She took her umbrella in case it rained.

What's the difference in meaning?

1 I'll buy some apples if I get hungry.
2 I'll buy some apples in case I get hungry.

PRACTICE

1 In pairs, match the items in the picture above with the phrases below to explain why you need certain things in your car.

get lost   break down in the dark
run out of petrol   have an accident
have a puncture

EXAMPLE
You need a spare can of petrol in case you run out (of petrol).

2 How would you use *in case* in these situations?

1 You hear a weather forecast which predicts that it will probably rain in your area just as you leave your home. What do you say?
2 You are talking to an American visitor. When you say goodbye, you give him/her your address. What do you say?

3 Complete these sentences with *if* or *in case*.

1 I'll take a plastic bottle of water . . . I get thirsty.
2 Can you buy me a newspaper . . . you pass a kiosk on your way home?
3 We'll have a swim . . . we see a nice place by the river.
4 I'll change a travellers' cheque . . . the bank is open.
5 He took some extra travellers' cheques . . . he ran out of money.
6 . . . the post office is open, can you buy me some stamps?
7 When you drive to the mountains this winter, put chains on your wheels . . . the roads are icy.

TALKING POINT

In pairs or groups, discuss what precautions concerning injections, money, medical supplies, clothing and equipment you need to take on a trip to one of the following places:

Lapland   The Sahara Desert   The Amazon

LISTENING

Listen to someone giving advice about a trip to Thailand. Note the advice she gives about luggage, clothes, money and learning the language.

WRITING

Some friends are going to spend a week in your home while you are away. Write a note welcoming them and explaining where and why you have left the following:
extra blankets, spare key, your phone number, your doctor's phone number.

Start like this:

Dear Mark and Jenny,

Welcome to the flat. You will find some extra blankets in the . . . in case . . .

— 20 —
Reading

'As soon as I got to Borstal, they made me a long-distance cross-country runner... running had always been encouraged in our family, especially running away from the police.'

The Loneliness of the Long-Distance Runner, a short novel by Alan Sillitoe, is about a boy at a Borstal school, which is a special centre for teenage boys who have committed crimes. The boy is a talented runner and on Sports Day the Governor of the Borstal wants him to win the long-distance race against another school.

Before you read
1 What do you think life at a Borstal school is like?
2 Find the meaning of these two adjectives in your dictionaries: *rebellious cooperative*. Which do you think a boy at Borstal is more likely to be?

The Loneliness of the Long-Distance Runner

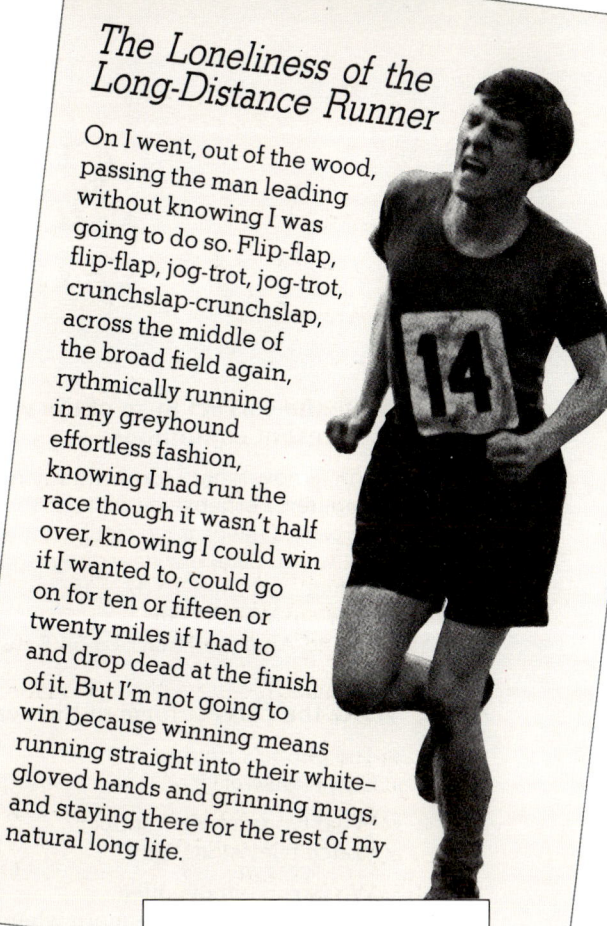

On I went, out of the wood, passing the man leading without knowing I was going to do so. Flip-flap, flip-flap, jog-trot, jog-trot, crunchslap-crunchslap, across the middle of the broad field again, rythmically running in my greyhound effortless fashion, knowing I had run the race though it wasn't half over, knowing I could win if I wanted to, could go on for ten or fifteen or twenty miles if I had to and drop dead at the finish of it. But I'm not going to win because winning means running straight into their white-gloved hands and grinning mugs, and staying there for the rest of my natural long life.

Glossary
greyhound a fast racing dog
mug (coll) face

COMPREHENSION
1 Read the extract on the right and choose (a), (b), or (c).

1 The best word to describe the boy is:
a) lazy b) rebellious
c) competitive.
2 The best word to describe the boy's running is:
a) wimpish b) macho
c) effortless.
3 The boy:
a) wins the race
b) wants to win the race
c) knows he can win the race.
4 The people with 'white-gloved hands and grinning mugs' are:
a) the boy's friends
b) his relatives
c) the police.

THINK ABOUT IT
Why doesn't the boy want to win the race?

TALKING POINT
What happens to young criminals in your country? Do you agree with the punishment they receive? Why? Why not?

STYLE
1 How many sentences are there in the text? Which is the longest sentence? What effect does it give?

2 Sounds can be conveyed by words, e.g. *clip clop, woof-woof, miaouw, buzz, ding dong.* Which of these words describe the sounds made by: *a dog, a church bell, a cat, a bee, horses' hooves*? How do you make and write these sounds in your language?

Which words in the text give the feeling of somebody running?

VOCABULARY
1 Find words or expressions in the extract which mean:

1 going ahead of somebody in a race
2 without needing to try hard
3 continue
4 smiling broadly

2 Phrasal verbs

A phrasal verb is formed by joining prepositions (e.g. *up, down, out* etc) or adverbs (e.g. *away, back,* etc) to the verb to make a new verb with a different meaning.

EXAMPLE
run away = escape.

Rewrite the following sentences using one of the phrasal verbs below.

run into   run away
run over   run off
run out of

1 The car nearly *hit* the cat.
2 I *met* an old school friend in the market today.
3 The deer *escaped* from the hunter.
4 I *haven't got* any milk *left*.
5 She *disappeared* with all the money.

Self check 2

Units 11–20

1 Write the correct form of the verbs in brackets, using the *going to* future or the present continuous.

1. I don't know what I (do) with my old computer. Perhaps you'd like it?
2. The plane (leave) at 6 o'clock.
3. I know you (like) our new geography teacher.
4. Come on! We (be) late.
5. Sue and Alan (get) married on Saturday.
6. Take a warm coat. It's very cloudy. I think it (snow).
7. I (take) my driving test on Wednesday.
8. The twins (arrive) on the 11.50 train.
9. I feel terrible. I think I (be) sick.
10. The new boutique (open) on 5th May.

2 Write the correct form of the verbs in brackets, using *will* or *going to*.

1. A: The phone's ringing.
   B: O.K. I (answer) it.
2. A: What (you/do) after supper?
   B: Watch television. Why?
3. A: We've run out of coffee.
   B: Have we? I (get) some more when I go out.
4. A: Have a good time in Italy!
   B: Thanks. I (send) you a postcard.
5. A: When (you/repair) my bike, Mum?
   B: I (do) it tomorrow if I have time.
6. A: Phew! It's hot in here.
   B: Yes, isn't it. I (turn on) the air conditioning.
7. A: Which do you want, the red one or the black one?
   B: I (have) the red one please.
8. A: It's so crowded in here I think I (faint).
   B: I (take) you outside for a while.

3 Write the correct form of the verbs in brackets using *will* or the present simple.

1. When she (hear) her result, she (be) pleased.
2. I (not phone) you unless something important (happen).
3. If he (not come), you (be) upset?
4. They (laugh) when they (realise) it's a trick.
5. I think you (like) Nick when you (meet) him.
6. I (send) you a postcard as soon as I (reach) Paris.
7. I (get) some fresh eggs if they (have) any in the market.
8. (Go) she to college if she (get) good grades in her exams?

4 Match the two halves of the following sentences.

1. If they find out about this
2. Here are some sandwiches
3. I won't call a doctor
4. You'll arrive before lunch
5. Will he take the job
6. It'll taste much nicer
7. Please don't telephone
8. If you soak it in cold water
9. I'll cook the spaghetti
10. I'll buy her some flowers

a) if you catch the 9.00 train.
b) there'll be trouble.
c) if they offer it to him?
d) the stain will come out.
e) in case you get hungry.
f) unless her temperature goes up.
g) when she's had her operation.
h) if you add a little sugar.
i) unless it's urgent.
j) as soon as they arrive.

Self check 2

5 Complete the sentences with *can, could* or the correct form of *be able to*. In some sentences more than one answer is possible.

1 If we're lucky we . . . see the whole match.
2 What? She's seven and she . . . (not) tie her shoelaces!
3 I'd like to . . . speak a little bit of every language.
4 I went to the library, Mrs Price, but I . . . (not) find the book you wanted.
5 After trying for many hours, they . . . to rescue the boy.
6 I . . . (not) swim until I was fifteen.

6 Circle the best answer.

1 A: Tea or coffee?
   B: a) Do you think you could give me some tea please?
      b) Tea, please.
      c) I want tea.

2 A: a) Lend me your newspaper, please.
      b) Excuse me, would you mind lending me your newspaper?
      c) Excuse me, can't you lend me your newspaper?
   B: Certainly.

3 A: It's Michael. He's phoning from the airport.
   B: Goodness!
      a) Has he left yet?
      b) Isn't he leaving yet?
      c) Hasn't he left yet?

4 A: I went out with Britta yesterday.
   B: I think I know her.
      a) She isn't the girl from the sports shop.
      b) Is she the girl from the sports shop?
      c) Isn't she the girl from the sports shop?
   A: That's right.

5 A: I remember you.
      a) You went to Kent High School, didn't you?
      b) Did you go to Kent High School?
      c) Aren't you going to Kent High School?

7 What would you say in the following situations? Sometimes there is more than one possible answer.

1 Your friend is out when you telephone so you want to leave a message.
2 You have bought a lot of stamps at the post office and you would like a receipt.
3 You are introduced to someone at a party. You are sure you went to school with him.
4 You offer a friend an ice cream but she refuses. Express surprise that she doesn't like ice cream.
5 Ask your teacher politely to give you extra grammar lessons.
6 Your mother returns home early one evening. You thought she was supposed to be at a meeting.
7 You are at a party. Give advice to a friend who spills red wine on a white carpet.
8 Your friend is going on holiday. You remind them to take out insurance.
9 You are going to spend a few days in France. Your friend loves French cheeses. What does the friend say to you?

Fluency 2

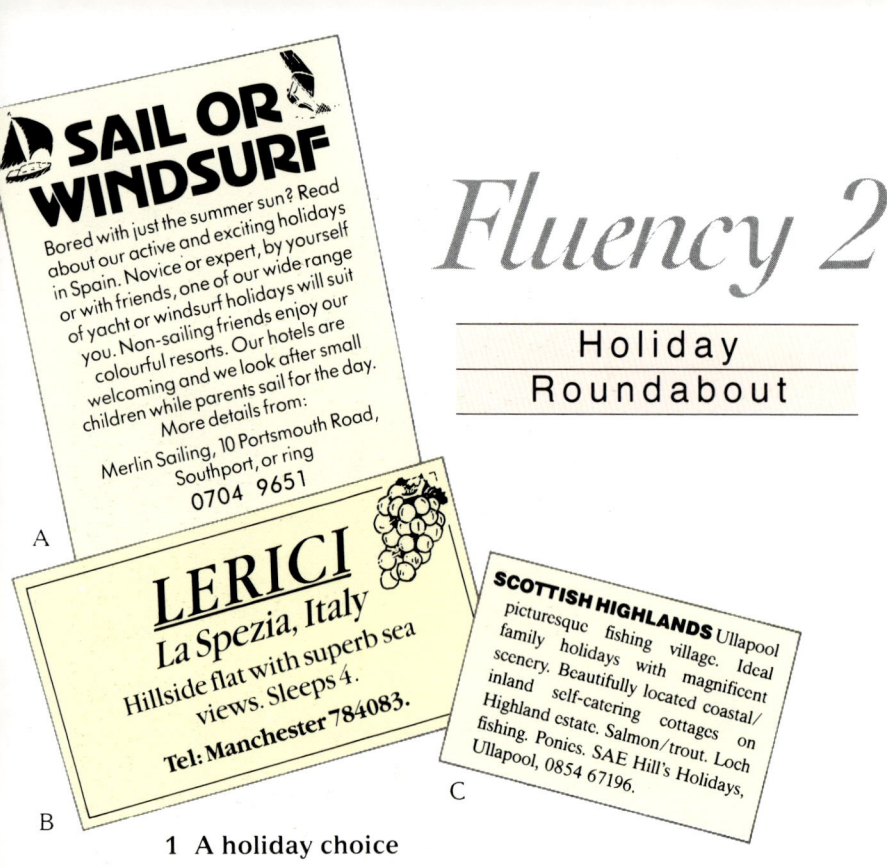

Holiday Roundabout

A
SAIL OR WINDSURF
Bored with just the summer sun? Read about our active and exciting holidays in Spain. Novice or expert, by yourself or with friends, one of our wide range of yacht or windsurf holidays will suit you. Non-sailing friends enjoy our colourful resorts. Our hotels are welcoming and we look after small children while parents sail for the day. More details from:
Merlin Sailing, 10 Portsmouth Road, Southport, or ring 0704 9651.

B
LERICI La Spezia, Italy
Hillside flat with superb sea views. Sleeps 4.
Tel: Manchester 784083.

C
SCOTTISH HIGHLANDS Ullapool picturesque fishing village. Ideal family holidays with magnificent scenery. Beautifully located coastal/inland self-catering cottages on Highland estate. Salmon/trout. Loch fishing. Ponies. SAE Hill's Holidays, Ullapool, 0854 67196.

1 A holiday choice

The Wood family are planning a two-week summer holiday. Look at the three holiday advertisements and the Wood family's preferences. Tick the holiday which best suits each person.

Name and preferences	Holiday A	Holiday B	Holiday C
Mr Wood 1 doesn't want to spend too much money. 2 doesn't like flying. 3 doesn't like too much sun.			
Mrs Wood 1 would like warm sunny weather. 2 would like to relax. 3 doesn't want to cook.			
Cara Wood 1 doesn't like staying in hotels. 2 likes Italian food. 3 wants to get a good tan.			
Jeff Wood 1 would like to practise his Spanish. 2 would like an active holiday. 3 likes a busy nightlife.			

2 A holiday discussion

In groups of four, act out a discussion between the members of the Wood family to agree on ONE of the holidays. In your discussion, use language like this:
I don't want to go to . . .
because it'll be/won't be . . .
If we go to . . ., I'll have to . . ./I won't be able to . . .

3 A holiday postcard

Write a postcard home to a friend. Say where you are and what you are doing. Say something about your plans for the next few days and when you are arriving back home. Ask your friend to meet you at the airport. Say what you'll do if he/she is not there.

4 A delay at the airport

On the way home, your plane is delayed. Act out a conversation with an airport official. Find out why there is a delay and how long you are going to have to wait. Ask what the airline is going to do about meals and hotel accommodation if the plane is delayed.

5 A game

After a sleepless night at the airport, you think about the things you are going to do when you get home. Say in turn what you are going to do, repeating what has been said before each time. If you don't remember, you must drop out of the game, e.g:
S1: When I get home, I'm going to have a lovely hot shower.
S2: When I get home, I'm going to have a lovely hot shower and then I'm going to have an ice cold orange juice.

Introducing *Glenn*

Look at the pictures of Glenn.
What nationality is he?
Why do you think he's visiting Britain?
What's special about Stratford?
What job do you think he has?
Do you think it's permanent or temporary?

Now read about Glenn.
Were you right?

ABOUT BRITAIN
Stratford-upon-Avon

Stratford-upon-Avon, a market town in Warwickshire, is the birthplace of England's most famous playwright and poet, William Shakespeare (1564–1616). It is one of the most popular and most famous attractions in Britain and is visited every year by over a million people.

-21-

Glenn

An American in Britain

Stratford-upon-Avon,
Warwickshire,
England

July 15

Dear Lori,

Sorry I haven't written for so long but I've been very busy. As you know, I've been working my way around Europe since I last wrote and I haven't had time to write home.

As you can see from my address, I've finally arrived in Stratford-upon-Avon. It really is a beautiful town, even though it's crawling with tourists. In fact, I've been standing in line at the theater for two hours trying to get a ticket to see 'Hamlet' and I've finally managed to get one. I'm really happy. They say it's a great play.

I'm really happy to be here in this and consider I've been over jus

I've just started a temporary job as a waiter in a hotel here. The chef is really strange! He got mad at me because I made a mistake with the breakfast orders and he hasn't stopped persecuting me since. I don't want to get fired. I really need to make some money this summer.

Are you still in NYC or have you managed to get to your place on Long Island yet? I hope the boat wasn't washed away in all those storms I've been hearing about.

I guess I'd better stop and get back to work. Be good and say Hi to the Empire State for me!

Love,
Glenn

P.S. Could you do me a favor and send me a copy of the Village Voice? I want to keep in touch.

Words to learn

finally chef temporary persecute
fired storm do somebody a favour

1 Read and find out:

1 where Glenn is now.
2 why he's feeling pleased.
3 what job he's got.
4 why he doesn't want to lose it.

Glossary
'Hamlet' a famous play by William Shakespeare, who was born in Stratford-upon-Avon
NYC New York City
Long Island a summer resort area just outside the city of New York
The Empire State the Empire State Building, a famous New York landmark
The Village Voice a weekly New York newspaper

UNIT 21: Glenn

2 Number the topics in the order in which they occur in Glenn's letter.

– a description of his job
– his recent travels
– an apology and a reason for not writing earlier
– his opinion of Stratford
– an incident which occurred at work
– an inquiry about life back in the USA
– a description of the chef in his job
– where Glenn is at the moment

3 Match the American English expressions with their British English equivalents.

AMERICAN ENGLISH	BRITISH ENGLISH
standing in line	holiday
guess	Hello!
movie	queuing
mad	think
vacation	film
Hi!	angry

4 About you

1 Have you ever worked in a restaurant or hotel? What was it like?
2 What sort of temporary jobs can foreigners get in your country? What sort of permit do they need?

VOCABULARY

1 The verb *to get*

The verb *to get* has many different meanings e.g.
to receive, to obtain,
to arrive (at).
When used with an adjective it means *to become*:
I'm getting tired. =
I'm becoming tired.

When used with a past participle, it can have a passive meaning:
I got fired. =
I was fired. (passive)
Get occurs mostly in informal English.

Complete the sentences below. Make sure the tense of the verb *get* is correct.

GET + PARTICIPLE	GET + ADJECTIVE
get fired	get tired
get drunk	get angry
get lost	get ready
get married	get better

1 Ann has been very ill but at last she's . . .
2 Barry and Amy have just announced that they're going to . . .
3 The reason they were late was because they . . .
4 I made a lot of spelling mistakes because I . . .
5 When she can't find a parking space, she always . . .
6 If you're late again, you'll . . .
7 They're coming in ten minutes. Please hurry up and . . .
8 Have a good time at the party but don't . . .

2 There are several different ways of pronouncing *ea* in English. Look at the list below.

GROUP 1
/iː/ eat

GROUP 2
/e/ breakfast

GROUP 3   GROUP 4
/eɪ/ break   /ɪə/ ear

3 Listen and write the following words in the correct sound group.

tea   real   year   speak
theatre (to) read dead
mean   dear   ready
steak pleased head
leave Shakespeare

LISTENING

An American student has just visited Stratford.

Note:
1 why she's in Britain.
2 what she thinks of the British theatre.
3 her impressions of Stratford.

TALKING POINT

List three arguments for or against living in places like Stratford-upon-Avon. In groups, discuss your arguments using the phrases below.

A: *The worst thing must be . . .*
   A big disadvantage must be . . .
   And what about the . . .
B: *Yes, but think of . . .*
   An advantage must be . . .

22

Grammar

Present perfect simple and continuous

What's the difference in meaning?
1 He's worked in Stratford.   2 He's been working in Stratford.

Which verb tense is used in each sentence? Look back at the text about Glenn in Unit 21. Find all the examples of these two tenses. Check the Focus section below to see the different ways in which the two tenses can be used.

FOCUS

The present perfect simple
This tense relates past events to present time. It is used
- to talk about experiences and events at an unspecified time in the past:
  I've seen two plays by Shakespeare.
  I've never been to Stratford.
- to talk about something that is unfinished:
  I've lived in Stratford for ten years.
- to talk about events in a period of time that is not yet finished, e.g. *this morning/week*:
  I've been to two parties this week.
- to talk about a present result of a past event:
  She's had an accident. She's broken her leg.

Note that it is often used in connection with certain words:
- the time prepositions *since* and *for*:
  She's lived here for three years.
  He's worked here since 1985.
- the adverbs *just* and *already*:
  I've just finished it.
  I've already done it.
  These adverbs are not generally used in negative sentences with the present perfect.
- the adverb *yet*
  Have you done it yet?
  I haven't done it yet.
  This adverb is not used in positive sentences with the present perfect.

The present perfect continuous
This tense is used
- to describe an action which began in the past and is either still going on, or has recently stopped. Compare:

  I've been writing letters all morning. (Present perfect continuous. The activity is important.)
  I've written three letters. (Present perfect simple. The letters are now finished.)
- It is often used with *for* and *since*:
  I've been living here for a few months/since September. (I am still living there.)

In which position in the sentence do the adverbs *just*, *already* and *yet* occur in the examples?

Identify the tenses in the short conversations below.

A: What did you do last night?
B: I read a book.

A: Why are your eyes sore?
B: I've been reading.

A: Do you want to borrow this book?
B: No thanks, I've read it.

UNIT 22: Grammar

PRACTICE

1 Ask and answer about personal experiences, using the present perfect and the past simple of the verbs in the phrases below.

EXAMPLE
A: Have you ever been to the USA?
B: No, I haven't. Have you?
A: Yes, I went there with my parents two years ago.

1 go to the USA
2 break an arm or leg
3 see a famous person in real life
4 write to a magazine or newspaper
5 win a competition
6 find anything valuable

2 Look at the pictures. Ask and answer questions using the present perfect continuous.

EXAMPLE
1 A: What have you been reading?
  B: I've been reading a romantic novel.

1 What? 2 What? 3 What? 4 What? 5 Who?

3 In pairs, ask and say how long you have been doing the things in the list below. Use *for* or *since* in your answers.

1 living in your present home
2 studying in this school or college
3 learning English
4 using this textbook
5 doing this unit

4 Tell your partner about the following:

1 a sport or activity you've been doing a lot of recently
2 a sport you haven't done for a long time
3 a book you've been reading
4 a country you've always wanted to visit

🔲 LISTENING

Lori has written a letter to Glenn from Long Island in the USA and spoken it onto a cassette. Listen to her letter-cassette and say:

what annual event has just taken place.
what the weather's been like.
what happened to their summer cabin.
what she's been doing recently.

WRITING

Before you write

Look at the expressions below. You are writing an informal letter. Which would you use to: 1) start the letter 2) introduce a new topic 3) close the letter?

By the way, . . .
Did you know that . . . ?
Thanks very much for your last letter.
Well, that's enough for now.
Sorry I haven't written before but . . .
It was great to get your letter.
Give my regards/love to . . .
Anyway, I'd better stop now.
Have you heard . . . ?
Best wishes, . . .
Say hello to . . .
Love from . . .

Write a letter

Write to an English-speaking penfriend. Start by apologising for not writing before and give a reason. Describe some of the things you have done or have been doing recently. Say what the weather has been like. Close the letter by sending greetings to any other people you know.

-23-

Communication

Making complaints

Before you read

What do you think the people are complaining about in the pictures above?

🔲 DIALOGUE

Glenn is serving dinner in the hotel restaurant.

At table 12:
WOMAN: Excuse me.
GLENN: Yes, madam?
WOMAN: I'm afraid I can't eat this steak. I asked for a medium steak and this is rare. In fact, it's almost raw. Could you change it for me, please?
GLENN: Yes, certainly. I'm sorry about that. I'll take it back to the kitchen.
WOMAN: Thank you.

At table 4:
MAN: Excuse me.
GLENN: Yes, sir?
MAN: It's very draughty here next to the door. I'd be grateful if you could find us another table.
GLENN: We're very busy today.
MAN: Couldn't we move to one of the tables in the corner?
GLENN: I'm afraid those are all reserved, sir.
MAN: Well, I'm sorry but we really can't sit here. Would you mind finding out if there are any other tables free?
GLENN: Yes, I'll go and ask right away.

Listen and answer the questions.

1 What does the woman ask Glenn to do? Why?
2 What does the man want Glenn to do? Why?

FOCUS

Complaints/requests

- Making complaints:
  I'm afraid I can't eat this steak. It's almost raw.
  I'm sorry but we can't sit here. It's very draughty.

- Requesting action:
  Could you change it please?
  Would you mind finding out?
  I'd be grateful if you could find us another table.

PRACTICE

1 Sort the words and phrases below into groups according to complaints about: automatic vending machines, hotel rooms, clothes and restaurant food.

doesn't work	zip broken
noisy	underdone
small	button missing
salty	gone wrong
dark	sweater shrunk
lining torn	broken down
cold	doesn't return coin
damp	overdone

Now use the words and phrases to practise making complaints.

2 In pairs, use the following situations to act out conversations.

1 You are in a restaurant and your hamburger is dry and overdone. You want the waitress to bring you another one.

2 You are in a hotel. Your room overlooks the rear car park and it is very noisy. Ask the receptionist to give you a different room.

3 You recently bought a pair of jeans but the first time that you wore them the zip broke. You take the jeans back to the shop to complain and ask for another pair in exchange.

4 You have put 50p into the automatic drinks machine to get a soft drink. The machine doesn't work and you have lost your 50p. You complain to one of the attendants and ask for your money back.

📞 LISTENING

Listen to the telephone conversations. Note what the callers are complaining about and what action they are requesting.

READING

1 Read the two advertisements.

Find out:
what two products are advertised.
which one is waterproof.
which one responds to your voice.
how much the products cost.

2 Read the letter of complaint below to a mail order company.

Find out which product the customer bought, what is wrong with it and what the customer wants the company to do.

WRITING

You ordered a radio cassette player from the mail order company and it arrived last week. It worked well until you went on holiday. Now the fast forward button doesn't work when you press it. Write a letter of complaint.

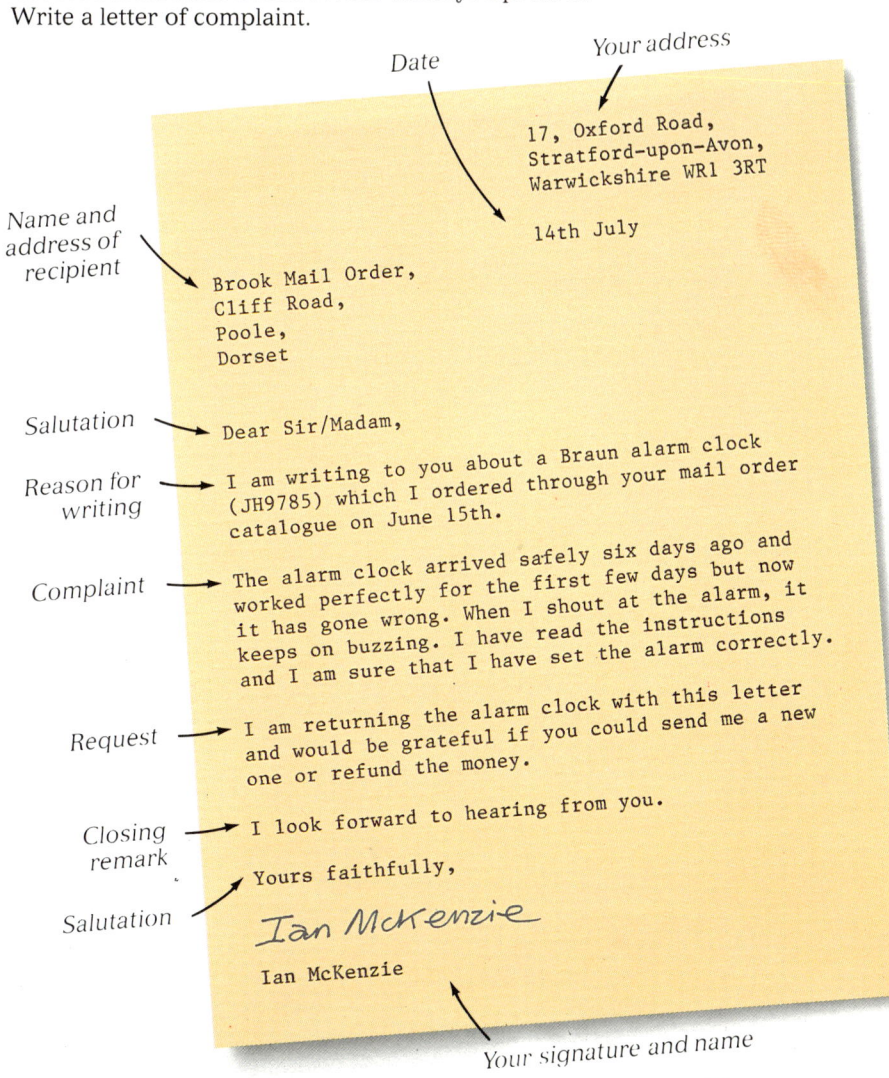

Alba water-resistant radio/cassette player with AM/FM stereo radio and fast-forward, stop and play controls. The mechanism and control keys are rubber-sealed to prevent damage from summer showers and winter snow.
Operates on 2 × R6 batteries (not supplied). Colour: Yellow.
FB5609 £34.99

Braun quartz battery operated, voice controlled, snooze alarm clock with three-stage increasing volume alarm. Talk to the clock and the alarm stops for four minutes then automatically restarts. Conventional finger tip on-off alarm control.
Height: 3in (7.5cm)
JH9785 £17.99

Your address → 17, Oxford Road,
Stratford-upon-Avon,
Warwickshire WR1 3RT

Date → 14th July

Name and address of recipient → Brook Mail Order,
Cliff Road,
Poole,
Dorset

Salutation → Dear Sir/Madam,

Reason for writing → I am writing to you about a Braun alarm clock (JH9785) which I ordered through your mail order catalogue on June 15th.

Complaint → The alarm clock arrived safely six days ago and worked perfectly for the first few days but now it has gone wrong. When I shout at the alarm, it keeps on buzzing. I have read the instructions and I am sure that I have set the alarm correctly.

Request → I am returning the alarm clock with this letter and would be grateful if you could send me a new one or refund the money.

Closing remark → I look forward to hearing from you.

Salutation → Yours faithfully,

Ian McKenzie

Ian McKenzie

Your signature and name

—24—

Grammar

Make and do

FOCUS

The verbs 'make' and 'do'
As you will see if you look in a dictionary, there are many uses of the verbs *make* and *do*. Here are some of them:

Make
- to create, produce or construct something:
  He made a delicious cake.
- to cause to be or happen:
  He made himself king.
  She made him angry.
- to force somebody to do something:
  She made him do his homework again.

Do
- to perform certain tasks and activities:
  He did his homework.
  I did the cleaning/housework/shopping/ironing/cooking.
- to perform actions which bring about a desired result:
  She's doing her hair/nails/room.
- to talk about progress:
  How is she doing at school?

Note
There are also certain fixed phrases with *make* and *do*:

Make
a mistake   your bed   sure (that)   an effort   a noise
an arrangement   money/love/war   your mind up

Do
your best   business   research   your duty   a deal
a degree/course   (someone) a favour   some work

Look in your dictionary and find two more fixed phrases with *make* and *do* to add to the list.

PRACTICE

1 Rewrite these sentences using an expression with *make*.

1 I've decided to leave my job.
2 They fixed a time to meet.
3 I'd like you to try hard to arrive on time in future.
4 You've done something wrong here.
5 You can't force me to go.
6 He earned a lot of money buying and selling houses.

2 Rewrite these sentences using *do*.

1 It only takes me a second to tidy my room.
2 She is coming on very well at art school.
3 We buy everything we need in the new supermarket.
4 Last year he was trading with the Soviet Union.

3 Write sentences using *make* or *do*.

Describe the following:

1 a job in the home you like doing.
2 a job in the home you hate doing.
3 something you like cooking.
4 something you have made for yourself or your home.
5 an arrangement or promise you have recently made.
6 when and where you are going to do your homework.

4 Compare your list with your partner's.

'I made a mistake with the breakfast orders.'

'Mr Partridge does the cooking.'

25

Reading

Hamlet
Prince of Denmark

Before you read
1 Have you ever seen a production of Shakespeare's famous tragedy, 'Hamlet'?
2 What do you know about the plot?

Words to learn
confused   ghost   murder (v)   proof
convinced   guilty   stab   drown
wound (v)   poison

COMPREHENSION
1 Reorder the paragraphs on the right to tell the story of 'Hamlet'.

2 Answer the questions.
1 Who is Hamlet?
2 Who is the ghost?
3 What does the ghost want Hamlet to do? Why?
4 Why does Hamlet kill Polonius?
5 How does Hamlet die?
6 How many people die and how?

3 Write True, False or Don't know.
1 After Claudius murdered his brother he married Gertrude and became king.
2 Hamlet planned to kill Polonius.
3 Ophelia drowned herself because Hamlet went to England.
4 Laertes knew that his sword was poisoned.
5 Gertrude took the cup of poison on purpose.

VOCABULARY
Which word does not belong in each group?

1 producer	doctor	director	actor
2 scene	act (n)	interval	box-office
3 chapter	musical	tragedy	comedy
4 stalls	balcony	circle	programme
5 orchestra	footlights	curtains	spotlights

WRITING
Write the story of a famous play or novel, using the present simple and the present perfect tense.

Start like this:
(Title of play/novel/poem)
... is a famous ... by .... It was written in ....
The story of ... is as follows:

---

a Ophelia's brother, Laertes, wants revenge for the deaths of his father and sister, so he challenges Hamlet to a duel. King Claudius gives Laertes a poisoned sword to use against Hamlet in the duel but the plan goes wrong and both Hamlet and Laertes are wounded by the same sword.

b Hamlet hears about the ghost and decides to see for himself. At midnight, the ghost appears and tells Hamlet that he was murdered by Claudius. The ghost makes Hamlet promise to take revenge for his murder and Hamlet agrees to kill Claudius.

c As the poison from the sword slowly begins to take effect on Hamlet and Laertes, Queen Gertrude drinks from a cup of poisoned wine which Claudius has prepared for Hamlet. As Laertes is dying, he tells Hamlet the truth about the poisoned sword. In the final scene, Hamlet stabs his uncle with the same sword just before he dies.

d Prince Hamlet is heir to the Danish throne and is in love with Ophelia, the daughter of Polonius, the Lord Chamberlain. Hamlet's father, the King of Denmark, suddenly dies. Hamlet's mother, Gertrude, immediately marries the dead king's brother, Claudius, who makes himself king. Hamlet is confused and deeply unhappy about these events. When the play opens, some guards are talking about a ghost they have seen on the castle walls. The ghost looks like Hamlet's father.

e However, Hamlet cannot make up his mind to do it. He wants proof of his father's murder and asks a group of actors to perform a play about the murder of a king by his brother. When Claudius sees the play, he rushes out of the room during the murder scene. Hamlet is now convinced that his uncle is guilty and goes to accuse his mother.

f Hamlet leaves for England, not realising that Claudius has secretly planned his murder during the journey. Meanwhile Ophelia, who has been rejected by Hamlet, drowns herself from grief in a stream. Hamlet manages to escape and returns to Denmark.

g While Hamlet is telling his mother that he knows the truth, he hears a noise behind a curtain. He thinks Claudius is secretly listening to their conversation. He stabs and kills the person behind the curtain who is, in fact, Polonius, Ophelia's father. Now King Claudius has a good excuse to send Hamlet away and he orders him to go to England.

−26−

Grammar

The passive

What's the difference in style?

1 They're building a new office block near our school.
2 An office block is being built near our school.

Which sentence is in the active and which is in the passive voice? Which sounds like something you would write in a report or a letter to a newspaper and which sounds like something you would say to a friend?

FOCUS

The passive

The passive is formed by combining the verb *to be* (in the tense required) with the past participle of the main verb.

Present simple:	is	
Present continuous:	is being	
Future:	will be	
Future *going to*: The musical	is going to be	performed ...
Past simple:	was	
Past continuous:	was being	
Present perfect:	has been	
Past perfect:	had been	

The passive is used

- to give factual information:
  The musical Cats is based on the poems of T.S. Eliot. It was composed by Andrew Lloyd Webber.

- when what is/was done is more important than who is doing/did the action:
  Wine from California is exported to France.

- to introduce general opinions:
  It is now recognised as one of the most successful musicals of all time.

- to express rules:
  Smoking is not allowed here.
  It is forbidden to walk on the grass.

- to describe processes:
  Bread is made from flour.

Note
In daily, informal language we tend to use the active voice. The passive voice is used more often in formal written English.

Look at the text about 'Cats' above and notice the tense of each of the verbs in the passive voice.

CATS

The musical 'Cats', which is based on the poems of T.S. Eliot, was composed by Andrew Lloyd Webber and directed by Trevor Nunn. It was first produced in London in 1981 and has been performed in over nineteen capital cities of the world, including Budapest, Tokyo and of course New York. It is now recognised as one of the most successful musicals of all time.

PRACTICE

1 Using a passive each time, give an example of where they grow, produce or make each of the items below.

EXAMPLE
Wine is produced in many parts of France.
VW cars are made in Germany.

wine	tea	vodka
oil	coffee	(Name) cars
rice	bananas	whisky

2 In pairs, ask and say where in your country they do the following:

1 grow wheat, rice or potatoes
2 rear cattle
3 manufacture leather goods
4 mine coal or other minerals
5 catch a lot of fish
6 grow other fruit and vegetables

EXAMPLE
A: Where is wheat grown in (name of country)?
B: It's grown in (name of region or area), I think.

UNIT 26: Grammar

3 Discuss your personal experiences using the present perfect passive and the past simple passive of the verbs in the phrases below.

EXAMPLE
A: Have you ever been stopped by the police?
B: No, I haven't but my brother has.
A: Really? Why?
B: He was stopped for speeding on the motorway.

1 stop by the police
2 interview on television
3 give a surprise party
4 fine for parking
5 search by customs
6 ask to give a speech
7 involve in a road accident

4 Look at the information on the right. Write complete passive sentences and say whether the statements are true or false. Correct those that you know are wrong.

EXAMPLE
1 The 'Penny Black', the world's first postage stamp, was issued on 6th May, 1840. (True)

Check your answers with your teacher.

LISTENING

Listen to someone describing an audition. Note:

1 what the audition was for.
2 what character he was usually cast as.
3 what part he thought he was auditioning for.
4 what he was told to prepare.
5 how the audition went.
6 if he was chosen for the part.

WRITING

Use your notes from the Listening exercise to write a letter from the man to a friend.

Start like this:

Dear . . .

*Did I tell you in my last letter that I was going to be auditioned for . . .?
Well, the audition was . . .*

1

The Penny Black, the world's first postage stamp, (issue) on 6th May 1840.

2

The Volkswagen Beetle (design) in the early 1930s by Ferdinand Porsche, who better (know) for his typewriters.

3

A crude form of the ball-point pen (invent) in 1888. Much later, in the 1930s, the ball-point pen (make) famous by two Hungarian brothers with the name 'Biro'.

4

In one year, over 440 litres of soft drinks (drink) by one person in the USA.

5

The Star Wars films all (make) in the USA.

6

The sound of a humming bird (produce) in its throat.

−27−

Topic

The USA

Before you read

1. What do you know about New York City?
2. Where is it situated?
3. What are some of its famous sights?
4. Have you ever been there? What impressed you most?

THE EMPIRE STATE BUILDING

NEW YORK CITY is situated at the mouth of the Hudson River on the East coast of the USA. It is made up of five boroughs with a combined population of over 17 million people. The heart of New York City is the island of Manhattan, where, in the Midtown and Downtown districts, the buildings 'scrape the sky'.

One of these skyscrapers is the Empire State Building on Fifth Avenue, between 33rd and 34th Street. Like the Statue of Liberty and Brooklyn Bridge, it is instantly recognised as a symbol of New York — a symbol which captures the power, energy and excitement of one of the world's most-loved and most-hated cities.

When the 102-storey stucture was built in 1931, it was the tallest building in the world. From the top, on a clear day, you can see over a 50-mile radius. Its towering height and distinctive Art Deco style made the Empire State Building an instant success with the public.

Its record as the world's tallest building has since been beaten — the World Trade Center in New York and the Sears Tower in Chicago are both taller — but the Empire State Building remains uniquely fascinating.

At night it is floodlit with coloured lights. Some people love the lights but others complain that their favourite New York building has been turned into the biggest Christmas tree in the world!

EMPIRE STATE FACTS

★ The Empire State is 'stepped' above a certain height, rather like a pyramid, to prevent it from blocking light and air from the neighbouring area.

★ There are 6,500 windows, nearly seven miles of elevator shafts and enough floor space to shelter a town of 80,000 people.

★ The building was first cleaned in 1962. It took thirty people six months to complete the job. They were all experienced at high altitudes, including one who was a former paratrooper.

★ In the famous film 'King Kong', the giant gorilla, King Kong, has his final battle from the top of the Empire State.

UNIT 27: Topic

Words to learn
district   scrape   instantly   symbol
power   energy   floodlit   prevent

1 Read and answer.

1 How many boroughs make up New York City?
2 Where exactly is the Empire State Building situated in Manhattan?
3 When was it built?
4 What happens to the building at night?
5 What happened in 1962?
6 Who was King Kong?

2 Correct the statements.

EXAMPLE
1 New York State is situated at the mouth of the Mississippi River.
No, New York State is situated at the mouth of the Hudson River.

2 In the downtown district of Manhattan the buildings are small and old-fashioned.
3 The Empire State Building is the tallest building in New York.
4 The Empire State was built in 1941.
5 It has never been cleaned.
6 The building is shaped like a tall rectangle.

3 About you

1 Have you ever been to the top of a high building? Did you feel faint or giddy?
2 Does any building or monument in your country fascinate you?
3 Can you name a place or building which is a symbol of your country?

VOCABULARY
Types of buildings

1 Sort the following into order of:

Height
a) block of flats   c) house
b) skyscraper   d) bungalow

Size
a) detached house   c) palace
b) cottage   d) hut

Privacy
a) semi-detached house
b) terraced house
c) detached house
d) one-bedroom flat

2 Which is the odd word out?

a) warehouse   b) factory   c) villa
d) office block

LISTENING

Listen to someone talking about how her original ideas about Americans and the USA — in particular New York — were altered by her visit.

Note:
what she thought before her visit.
what she thinks now.

TALKING POINT

Discuss briefly how the following have influenced the world and say which you approve and disapprove of.

Walt Disney   Martin Luther King
hamburgers   Hollywood films
rock music   blue jeans
Ronald Reagan   skyscrapers
TV crime series   Henry Ford
Marilyn Monroe   soap operas
space exploration

WRITING

Write a description of a famous building, monument or landmark in your country.

PARAGRAPH 1
Say what the building is and where it is situated. Say when it was built and who it was designed by.

PARAGRAPH 2
Describe the building and any distinctive features.

PARAGRAPH 3
Give any other information about the building which makes it famous.

EXAMPLE
A very famous building in . . . is . . ., situated in . . . It was built in . . . and was designed by the famous architect, . . .
   One of its main attractions is . . . It is/was here that . . .

Speech bubbles in photo:
- Do we have to stay to the end?
- Don't forget. You're expected to make a speech.
- I think we should thank the vicar.
- Am I supposed to look happy?

—28—

Communication

Obligation and prohibition

FOCUS

Obligation and prohibition

- Ask about obligation:
  Do we have to stay to the end?
  Do you think we should take some flowers?
  Am I expected to make a speech?
  Am I supposed to look happy?

- Talk about obligation:
  I think we should thank the vicar.
  You're expected to make a speech.
  You're supposed to wear a hat.

- Talk about prohibition:
  You're not supposed to smoke.
  You mustn't/shouldn't talk loudly in church.

PRACTICE

1 In pairs, ask and say what you think you should do in the following social situations.

EXAMPLE
1 A teacher/class friend is leaving after a long time.
  A: What do you think we should do about Mrs Webster?
  B: I think we should collect some money for a present.

2 An elderly friend of the family is in hospital.
3 You are invited to a friend's wedding.
4 You are asked to lunch at your friend's parents' house.
5 A friend of the family dies.
6 You are inviting a Hindu family to a meal.

2 In pairs, complete the questionnaire below about polite behaviour in your country.

EXAMPLE
A: Do men have to wear jackets and ties in restaurants?
B: It depends on the restaurant. You don't have to in most restaurants but you're expected to wear a jacket and tie in expensive places.

3 Compare your answers with other pairs'.

Etiquette

A questionnaire

About clothing
1 Do men have to wear jackets and ties in restaurants?
2 Are men and women allowed to wear shorts to work in offices in summer?
3 Are there any special rules about what you have to wear in holy places?

About money
4 Is it rude to ask people how much money they earn?
5 Is a woman expected to pay her share of the bill in a restaurant?

About hospitality
6 Should you take a present when you are invited to somebody's home?
7 Is it rude to smoke without asking in other people's homes?
8 Is it impolite to smoke between courses?

About tipping
9 How much should you tip a taxi driver?
10 Is it the same in a restaurant and at the hairdresser's?

UNIT 28: Communication

ABOUT BRITAIN

Table manners

Although rules regarding table manners are not very strict in Britain, it is considered rude to eat and drink noisily. At formal meals, the cutlery is placed in the order in which it will be used, starting from the outside and working in. The dessert spoon and fork are usually laid at the top of your place setting, not at the side.

After each course, the knife and fork should be laid side by side in the middle of the plate. This shows that you have finished and the plate can be removed. If you leave the knife and fork apart, it will show that you have not yet finished eating.

It is considered impolite to smoke between courses unless your hosts say otherwise. It is polite to ask permission before you smoke in people's homes.

In Britain, smoking is now forbidden in many public places, e.g. on the underground, on stations, in shops, in theatres and in cinemas.

LISTENING

Listen to an American explaining American etiquette on table manners. Answer the following questions.
1 What is a man supposed to do before sitting down at the dinner table?
2 In which hand do Americans hold their fork?
3 When do they use their knife?
4 Where do they place the knife afterwards?

WRITING

Look at the example below, then write a few paragraphs about etiquette for visitors to your country. Give helpful advice about things like table manners, hospitality and tipping.

> Table Manners
>
> At mealtimes in Sweden we don't use side plates for bread. You're supposed to put your bread on the table beside your dinner plate. After a meal, you're expected to thank the person who prepared it, even if it's your mother or father.

TALKING POINT

Discuss which of the following habits you consider rude and why.
Which of them, if any, do you consider acceptable only at home, and
which do you consider completely unacceptable?

– helping yourself to food without asking
– starting to eat before everyone is served
– picking at food with your hands
– reading at the meal table
– resting your elbows on the table
– reaching across the table in front of people
– leaving the table before other people have finished
– not thanking the cook
– wiping your plate clean with bread

ACT IT OUT

You are on a trip to Britain and you have been invited to dinner with a British family. In pairs or groups, act out the conversation when you ask your teacher before the event what you are supposed to do. Ask about clothes, forms of address, times to arrive and leave, gifts to take and how to thank your hosts.

— 29 —

Grammar

This is a baker who gave me some fresh bread when I was hungry.

The dog which followed me all over the Lake District.

These are some fishermen I met when I was in South Shields.

The man whose cauliflowers won first prize in the Flower Show.

Clovelly, the village where I stayed in Devon.

Defining relative pronouns

FOCUS

Defining relative clauses with 'who' 'which' 'that' 'where' and 'whose'.

1 *Who/that* as a subject pronoun
- These are used in defining relative clauses to define the person or people we are talking about:
This is a baker who/that gave me some fresh bread.

2 *Which/that* as subject pronouns
- These are used in the same way to define things or places:
This is the dog which/that followed me all over the Lake District.

3 *Who, which, that* as object pronouns
- When the person or thing is the object of the verb in the relative clause, you can leave out *who, which* or *that*:
These are some fisherman (who/that) I met when I was in South Shields.

4 *Whose*
- *Whose* means *of whom* and replaces *his, her* and *their* in relative clauses. It can never be left out:
That's the man whose cauliflowers won first prize in the flower show.

5 *Where*
- This means *in which* and is used to talk about places. It can never be left out.
This is the village where I stayed in Devon.

PRACTICE

1 Join the sentences with *who, whose, which* or *that*.

EXAMPLE
1 A man lent me his hammer. He lives next door.
   The man who lives next door lent me his hammer.

2 A girl fainted. She was standing behind me in the queue. (The girl . . .)
3 Have you met the family? They have just moved in to the house next door. (Have you met . . .)
4 A man telephoned me this morning. His company sells computers.
5 What was the name of the car? It won the Car of the Year award.

2 Join the two sentences, omitting *who* or *which*.

EXAMPLE
1 That's the man. I was talking about him last night.
   That's the man I was talking about last night.

2 Did you like the photo? I took it of you and your husband. (Did you . . .)
3 What did you do with the eggs? I bought them this morning. (What did . . .)
4 You spoke to a man on the phone. That was my father. (The man . . .)
5 They bought a house. It was very expensive. (The house . . .)

3 Match the phrases and the sentences below, then join them to make one sentence, using *where*.

EXAMPLE
1 That's the hotel . . .
   That's the hotel where my sister spent her honeymoon.

2 Last night I went to a restaurant . . .
3 Over the road is the hairdresser's . . .
4 Why don't you go to the garage . . .
5 I went back to the part of the beach . . . but I couldn't find it.
6 That's the library . . .

A I usually have my hair cut there.
B My sister spent her honeymoon there.
C You can eat as much as you like for £10 there.
D I lost my watch there.
E They usually have interesting art exhibitions there.
F I take my car to be serviced there.

4 In pairs, ask about and identify the people in the picture. Use *who* or *whose* and choose from the character descriptions below.

EXAMPLE
A: Who's the girl in the red dress?
B: That's Ann. She's the one I told you about who overslept and missed the plane home.

ANN	She overslept and missed the plane home.
SALLY	Her bed broke in the middle of the night.
MARK	He stayed in his hotel room most of the day.
LUCY	She went out with one of the hotel waiters.
ROBERT	His wallet was stolen on the beach.
JAN	Her hotel room caught fire.
GORDON	His back got badly sunburnt.

WRITING

Write a paragraph describing in detail one of the items below. See how many relative clauses you can use.

– the last book you read
– a film you saw recently
– a supermarket where you usually do your shopping
– a town you like very much

How to be an alien

THE LANGUAGE

When I arrived in England I thought I knew English. After I'd been here an hour, I realised I did not understand a word.

THE WEATHER

You must never contradict anybody when discussing the weather. Should it hail and snow, should hurricanes uproot the trees from the side of the road, and should someone remark to you: 'Nice day, isn't it?' — answer without hesitation: 'Isn't it lovely!'

QUEUEING

An Englishman, even if he is alone, forms an orderly queue of one. At weekends an Englishman queues up at the bus stop, travels out to Richmond, queues up for a boat, then queues up for tea, then queues up for ice cream, then joins a few more odd queues just for the fun of it, then queues up at the bus stop and has the time of his life.

PETS

If you go out for a walk with a friend, don't say a word for hours; if you go out for a walk with your dog, keep chatting to him.

SEX

Continental people have a sex life; the English have hot-water bottles.

HOW TO PLAN A TOWN

1 First of all, never build a street straight.
2 Give a different name to a street whenever it bends.
3 Call streets by various names: street, road, place, mews, crescent, avenue, lane, way, park, gardens, path, walk, broadway, promenade, gate, terrace, view, hill etc.

'Nice day, isn't it?'   'Isn't it lovely!'

TEA

The trouble with tea is that originally it was quite a good drink. So a group of the most eminent British scientists put their heads together, and made complicated biological experiments to find ways of spoiling it.

They suggested that if you do not drink it clear but pour a few drops of cold milk into it, and no sugar at all, the desired object is achieved. Once this refreshing, aromatic, oriental beverage was successfully transformed into colourless and tasteless gargling water, it suddenly became the national drink of Great Britain and Ireland.

There are some occasions when you must not refuse a cup of tea. If you are invited to an English home, at five o'clock in the morning a cup of tea is brought in by a heartily smiling hostess. You have to declare with your best five o'clock smile: 'Thank you so much. I do adore a cup of early morning tea, especially early in the morning.' If you are left alone with the liquid, you may pour it down the washbasin.

Then you have tea for breakfast; then you have tea at eleven o'clock in the morning; then after lunch; then you have tea for tea; then after supper; and again at eleven o'clock at night.

Glossary
Richmond an attractive town on the river Thames
has the time of his life has a marvellous time
beverage drink
gargling liquid liquid to wash inside the throat and mouth

−30−
Reading

How to be an alien was written by George Mikes (pronounced /mikeʃ/), a Hungarian who came to live in Britain. It was first published in 1946 and has since been reprinted over forty times.

George Mikes said his book was meant: 'chiefly for xenophobes (people who dislike foreigners) and anglophobes (people who dislike England and the English).' The extract on the left includes some of the observations which have delighted generations of readers.

Guess the meaning
alien   contradict
hurricane   eminent
complicated   experiment
spoil   refreshing
aromatic   transform   adore

COMPREHENSION

Read the text above and the extract on the left and answer the questions.

1 Where did George Mikes come from?
2 When was *How to be an alien* first published?
3 What sort of book is it?
4 What does George Mikes say about the English
   – language?
   – attitude to the weather?
   – habit of queueing?
   – attitude to pets?
   – attitude to sex?
   – towns?
   – way of serving tea?
   – tea-drinking habits?

VOCABULARY

Adjective formation with *-less* and *-ful*

The suffix *-less* means *without*, e.g. *colourless* = *without colour*.
The suffix *-ful* means *with*, e.g. *colourful* = *with colour*

1 Combine a noun from the box with *-less* to make adjectives which describe the definitions below.

heart   care   pain   shape   home   use   job   thought

EXAMPLE
1 people who have nowhere to live
homeless

2 people who are cruel and unkind
3 people who are inattentive and don't take care
4 people who don't think about what they say or do
5 something which doesn't hurt
6 something that has no form
7 something that is broken or has no value
8 people who are out of work

Which of these adjectives can also be used as a noun to apply to people, in the same way as *the rich* and *the poor*?

2 Which of the nouns in Exercise 1 can be combined with *-ful* to make an adjective?

3 Sort the adjectives below into two groups to indicate a positive or a negative opinion.

true	silly	affectionate
funny	rude	xenophobic
stereotypical	superficial	old-fashioned
cruel	perceptive	witty

Which of them would you use to describe George Mikes's comments?

📼 LISTENING

Before you listen

Read the dictionary entry for a definition of *stereotype*.

> **ster·e·o·type¹** /ˈsteriətaɪp/ *n* [(**of**)] *usu. derog* (someone or something that represents) a fixed set of ideas about what a particular type of person or thing is like, which is (wrongly) believed to be true in all cases: *She believes that she is not a good mother because she does not fit the stereotype of a woman who spends all her time with her children.* | *The characters in the film are just stereotypes with no individuality.* | *racial stereotypes*
> —**·typical** / steriəʊˈtɪpɪkəl/ *adj*

Listen

Some people are discussing a joke based on national stereotypes of the Scots, the Irish and the English.

Note:
what national characteristics are implied in the joke.
how the Irishman felt about the joke.
what other types of joke the people thought were perhaps more offensive.

TALKING POINT

What are your views about the British? Make a note of your views on the following subjects:
– language
– attitude to work
– attitude to foreigners
– food
– dress sense
– homes
– behaviour/manners
– young people

How many of your views are positive, and how many are negative? Compare your opinions in groups. How many of your opinions are the same? Do you think this means they are stereotypes?

WRITING

Write paragraphs about national stereotypes. Say if you think they are true or not.

Many people think/say that the (name of nationality) are . . . . This is probably because . . . . In fact, ...

The (name of nationality) are said/thought to . . . because . . . but most of the people I know . . . .

Jokes are often made about us because we . . . and in some ways I think this is true.

A popular view of . . . is that we all . . . but actually . . . .

'And will you be going to Cruft's this year as usual, Florence?'

Self check 3

Units 21–30

1 Complete the parts of these irregular verbs.

EXAMPLE
break – broke – broken

1 break   3 spend   5 bring   7 spill   9 drive   11 give
2 fall   4 steal   6 speak   8 take   10 see   12 write

2 Write the correct form of the verbs in brackets, using the past simple or the present perfect simple tenses.

1 A: When (you/buy) the compact disc player?
  B: I (buy) it last week.
2 A: What (you/do) to your hair? It looks great.
  B: I (just/have) a haircut.
3 A: (You/ever/be) to America?
  B: Yes, I (go) there last year.
4 A: (You/see) my glasses? I can't find them.
  B: When (you/have) them last?
5 A: You must write and thank Aunt Julie for her present.
  B: I (already/write).
6 A: Oh no! I (spill) chocolate milkshake all down my jacket.
  B: I'll get a cloth.

3 Insert the correct form of *make* or *do* in the sentences.

1 Could you . . . me a cup of tea?
2 I haven't . . . my homework yet.
3 The business isn't . . . very well at the moment.
4 We would like everyone to . . . their beds every day and to . . . some cleaning.
5 Did you hear that they . . . her president of the club?
6 Try not to . . . a noise when you go upstairs.

4 Complete the conversation choosing from the sentences on the right.

YOU: (1) . . . ?
GLENN: Oh travelling around Europe for a bit and doing odd jobs here and there.
YOU: (2) . . . ?
GLENN: What? Here in Stratford? Oh, for a few days.
YOU: (3) . . . ?
GLENN: Yes, I have. In a hotel.
YOU: (4) . . . ?
GLENN: It's just a small one. You won't know it.
YOU: (5) . . . ?
GLENN: Yes, I've seen 'Hamlet' and 'King Lear'.
YOU: (6) . . . ?
GLENN: Yes, I did, especially 'Hamlet'.
YOU: (7) . . . ?
GLENN: Yes, I've been to see Anne Hathaway's Cottage and Shakespeare's birthplace.
YOU: (8) . . . ?
GLENN: Yes, I have. It's a great place, Stratford!

A: Have you been working?
B: Well you sound as if you've been enjoying yourself.
C: What have you been doing this summer?
D: Which hotel have you been working in?
E: Did you enjoy them?
F: And have you done any sightseeing?
G: How long have you been here?
H: Have you seen any Shakespeare plays yet?

5 Write the correct form of the verbs in brackets, using the passive.

1 A lot of apples (grow) in Normandy in France.
2 Meat (export) by Argentina to the rest of the world.
3 The forests of Northern Europe (destroy) slowly by acid rain.
4 'Hamlet' (write) by Shakespeare.
5 Do you know how President Abraham Lincoln (assassinate)?
6 The homework for the last lesson (not correct) yet.
7 Guess what! I (invite) to Jessica's party.

6 Choose the correct tense (the present simple passive or present continuous passive) and then rewrite the sentences.

1 A: Waiter, is my food ready? I'm in a hurry.
  B: It won't be long, sir. It's *cooked/being cooked* at the moment.
2 A: Is this bag plastic or leather?
  B: Madam, it's *being made/made* of the finest Italian leather.
3 A: Where's your car?
  B: It's *being repaired/repaired*.
4 A: Why are the children *sent/being sent* to bed?
  B: Because they've been naughty.
5 A: How are you all getting home from the airport?
  B: We're *being met/met* by my father.

7 Complete the paragraph by inserting relative pronouns where necessary.

Aesop was a Greek writer . . . probably lived in the 6th century B.C. Little is known about his life. He wrote fables (short stories . . . teach a particular lesson). Most of the fables . . . he wrote are about animals . . . speak and act like people. A fable . . . most people have read is called 'The Hare and the Tortoise'.

8 Circle the best sentences.

1 A: Can I help you?
  B: a) I'm sorry the zip on this shirt is broken.
     b) Yes, I'm afraid the zip on this shirt is broken.
     c) This zip is breaking.
2 B: a) Would you mind changing it please?
     b) Do you mind if you change it please?
     c) Please change it.
  A: No, not at all.
3 A: The invitation looks very formal.
     a) Do you think I must wear a dress?
     b) Do you think I should wear a dress?
     c) Do I expect to wear a dress?
4 A: Do we really have to go to the wedding?
  B: a) Yes, I think we're allowed to go.
     b) Yes, we had to go.
     c) Yes, I think we're expected to go.

9 Rearrange the jumbled sentences below and write a letter of complaint. Start your letter with *Dear Sir/Madam,*.

1 Could you also let me know if you would like the stereo returned.
2 A month ago I ordered a personal stereo from your firm.
3 I look forward to hearing from you.
4 There are several marks on it and one of the buttons doesn't work.
5 When it arrived, I found that the stereo had been damaged in the post.
6 I would be grateful if you could replace it or give me a refund.

Fluency 3

Celebration time

Imagine you are approaching the time of a festival or celebration such as Christmas, Easter, or Thanksgiving which is celebrated traditionally with special meals, customs and games.

1 A special festival

Listen to Joanne, an American, describing how Thanksgiving Day is celebrated. Note:
1 why and when it is celebrated.
2 how her family celebrate it.
3 what special food is eaten.
4 why Joanne thinks the occasion is special.

2 A conversation

Choose a festival from your country. In pairs, act out a conversation. One of you is an English-speaking guest. Ask about the festival, e.g. its name, when and how it is celebrated and what it means. The other person must describe the festival and give details of any customs and etiquette which the English guest should observe.

3 A letter of invitation

Write a letter to a British or an American friend inviting him/her to come and celebrate a special festival with you and your family. Use the information from the activity above and explain what happens and why you think your friend will enjoy it.

4 An argument

You have invited your boy/girlfriend to a family party and he/she arrives very late.

YOU
Your boy/girlfriend was supposed to arrive at your house at 8 p.m. He/She didn't turn up until 10 p.m. You are furious. You tell him/her how long you've been waiting, how worried you've been, and you demand an explanation. You suspect that he/she has been to see someone else and you are determined to find out.

GIRL/BOYFRIEND
You were asked to do some extra work for your boss and weren't allowed to leave until 7 p.m. The traffic was much busier than usual that evening. You try to convince your boy/girlfriend that you tried to get there as fast as possible.

5 A faulty gift

Act out and then write a conversation between a customer and a shop assistant about a faulty camera.

CUSTOMER
You bought an underwater camera as a birthday present for a friend. After two or three times in the water the camera started to leak (to let in water). You have taken the camera back to the shop where you bought it. You would like them to give you a new camera or at least to repair it free of charge.

THE SHOP ASSISTANT
A customer complains about a faulty camera. You want to know what the fault is, when the camera was bought, and if it has been dropped or damaged in any way. Before you agree to send the camera away to be repaired, you would like to see the receipt or some proof that the camera was bought in your shop.

Introducing Eve

Look at the pictures of Eve.
How old do you think she is?
What do you think she does for a living?
Where does she live?
What's special about the part of Britain which she lives in?
Why do you think she lives there?

Now read about Eve. Were you right?

LOCAL CRAFT IS ALIVE AND WELL

Eve
A jewellery maker

John Marsham meets Eve Maxwell, a 26-year-old jewellery maker from Avebury in Wiltshire

I FIRST MET Eve Maxwell in a covered market in Bath, where she has a stall. As we chatted, some people gathered, fingering the silver necklaces, bracelets and earrings on display. Eve had her eye constantly on the stall. 'If you turn your back for a moment, you can lose the lot.'

I asked her if she worked only in silver. 'Yes, silver fascinates me. I like the feel and look of it.' Eve makes her jewellery in a small cottage in Avebury, a village set in the high chalk downs of North Wiltshire. We drove back there after the market closed. 'I first came here when I was a student at art school. We had to do some sketches of the prehistoric stones. I fell in love with the place immediately. It's so peaceful. I'd go mad if I had to live in London.'

'Another good reason for living here is financial. If I had a market stall in London, in Portobello Road for example, I'd have to pay an enormous rent and it would cut my profits considerably.

'You have to be quite tough to set up your own business, particularly as a jeweller. Some stall holders are quite unscrupulous, especially in the antique side of the business. They don't put price tags on anything and they charge what they like if they think a customer will pay it. I couldn't do that. If I were a man, I'd probably be more aggressive about selling, but I do well enough. I also take commissions from people who want something special designed and made.

'My parents would prefer me to get a full-time job but I'd lose my independence if I did that. I enjoy being my own boss. I may not make a fortune but at least I can choose the hours I work. Besides, I love the creative part of the work. I would hate to work in an office all day.'

Words to learn
constantly fascinate
financial tough
unscrupulous aggressive
independence

1 Read and answer.
1 Where did the reporter first meet Eve?
2 What sort of jewellery does Eve sell?
3 Where does she live?
4 When did she first visit Avebury? Why?
5 What are Eve's reasons for not living in London?
6 Apart from selling jewellery on the stall, how else does she make money?
7 Why does she like her job?

Glossary
Wiltshire a county (an administrative district) in south-west England
chalk downs rounded hills of chalk
Portobello Road a street market specialising in antiques, jewellery and clothes

2 Read and think.

1 Why do you think that Eve 'had her eye constantly on the stall'?
2 Why do you have to be tough to set up your own business?
3 What is wrong with not having price tags?
4 What impression do you get of Eve?

3 About you

1 Are there any interesting markets you go to? What special things can you buy there?
2 Would you like to go into business on your own? Why/why not?

4 Read about Britain.

What's special about Avebury?

ABOUT BRITAIN

Avebury

Avebury is an attractive village in Wiltshire with an ancient church, an Elizabethan manor house and a collection of pretty cottages. It is surrounded by a stone circle called the 'Avebury Ring', one of the most important prehistoric monuments in Britain. The circle of stones was built by Bronze Age people over 2,000 years ago. Together with Stonehenge, it is part of a group of prehistoric monuments stretching from southern England to the north-eastern tip of Scotland. Some of the stones at Avebury weigh over forty tons. The purpose of the circle is unknown but it was probably an open-air temple or place of worship.

VOCABULARY

1 Find words or expressions from the text about Eve which have the same meaning as the following:

talk informally   all the time   drawings
related to money   hard (of people)   dishonest

2 Where do you wear the following?

EXAMPLE
1 You wear earrings on/in your ears.
1 earrings   4 brooch   7 ring
2 cuff-links   5 bracelet   8 gold chain
3 necklace   6 pendant   9 watch

3 In pairs, describe any jewellery you are wearing. Do you have a favourite piece of jewellery? If so, what is it?

4 Use a dictionary to find out how the following words are pronounced and write them in sound groups, e.g. *tough* /tʌf/.

though   brought   thought
bought   cough   although
nought   enough   ought
rough   fought   through

5 Now listen to the tape and see if you were right.

LISTENING

Before you listen

Look these words up in a dictionary:

tweezers, file, pliers, pincers, scissors

Listen

Listen to Phil, a jewellery maker, talking about his job. Then listen again and each time you hear the bleep, note down the question which you think the interviewer asked.

TALKING POINT

1 What is most important for you in a job? Write the following in order of importance, and add any other aspects which are important to you.

travel   money
your colleagues   holidays
being your own boss   the hours
meeting people   chance of promotion
variety   job satisfaction
working conditions   perks (e.g. car, lunch)

2 In groups, talk about your list.

WRITING

Linking devices: listing reasons

Choose a job which you would like to do and write a paragraph about the reasons why you would like to do it. Use the linking devices below to help you.

EXAMPLE
The main reason for wanting/choosing to be a travel courier is because it's a way of seeing the world. *Another good reason* is that you get a chance to meet lots of different people. *Besides*, I enjoy travelling.

Grammar

Second conditional *if* clauses

What's the difference in meaning?

1. I'll lose my independence if I get a full-time job.
2. I'd lose my independence if I got a full-time job.

What differences are there in the verb tenses between the two sentences? Which sentence is a 'first conditional' and which is a 'second conditional'?

Find more examples of the second conditional from the text about Eve. Are they all used in the same way? Check by looking at the Focus section below.

> ### FOCUS
> **The second conditional**
>
> This structure is used
> - to talk about hypothetical but possible situations:
>   *If I had a stall in London, I'd have to pay an enormous rent.*
>
> - to talk about totally imaginary or impossible situations:
>   *If I were a man, I'd probably be more aggressive.*
>
> - to give advice:
>   *If I were you, I'd get a full-time job.*
>
> **Points to note**
> - *Would* never occurs in the *if* clause.
>
> - The verb in the *if* clause is always in the past tense even though it refers to future or present time.
>
> - *Were* is often used instead of *was* after *if*, especially in written English:
>   *If he were here, he'd...*
>   *Was* often occurs in informal spoken English.

PRACTICE

1 Discuss the following situations with your partner.

1. What would you do if you won £100? £1,000? £10,000?
2. Who would you like to be if you woke up tomorrow as a different person?
3. What three things would you take with you if you were shipwrecked on a desert island?
4. Which single item would you save if your house/flat caught fire?

EXAMPLE
A: What would you do if you won £100?
B: I think I'd buy .../invest it in .../spend it on .../give it to ...

2 In pairs, imagine that one of you is a tourist visiting your town or city for the day. Practise asking for and giving the best advice in the following situations. Start your questions with:

Where/What can I ...
What/How do you think I should ...

EXAMPLE
A: Excuse me.
   Where can I buy a good map of the town?
B: If I were you, I'd go to ...

You want to know:
1. where to buy a good map of the town.
2. what important sights to see.
3. the best way of getting around the tourist sights.
4. what local food dishes to try.
5. the best place to change money.

3 In pairs, ask and answer the questions to complete the questionnaire on the opposite page for your partner. Then check your scores to find out how assertive he/she is.

UNIT 32: Grammar

HOW ASSERTIVE ARE YOU?

What would you do in these situations?

Complete the questionnaire and check your scores.

	Yes	No
1 If someone lit up a cigarette in a non-smoking area, would you tell them to put it out?		
2 If someone parked their car in your parking space, would you ask them to move it?		
3 If you were in a shop and wanted change for a £10 note, would you buy something small first before asking for change?		
4 If you badly wanted a glass of water while you were in town, would you go into a restaurant and ask for it?		
5 If a group of friends wanted you to go out with them, would you do so, even if you felt too tired?		
6 If you were late for a flight, would you go to the front of the check-in queue without waiting your turn?		
7 If someone pushed in front of you in a queue at the bank, would you say something to them?		
8 If you bought a pair of shoes and the heels came loose after a week, would you take them back to the shop and complain?		
9 If you weren't enjoying a play at the theatre, would you stay until the end?		
10 If a good friend asked to borrow a large sum of money, would you lend it if you had it?		

SCORING
Questions 1,2,4,6,7,8   Yes = 2 points   No = 0 points.
Questions 3,5,9,10   No = 2 points   Yes = 0 points.
The higher your score, the more assertive you are.

Fourteen or over: You have a strong personality. You insist on other people respecting your rights. Some people may think you are 'pushy' and aggressive.
Eight or under: You have a submissive personality and like to follow rather than to lead. People often take advantage of your good nature.

ACT IT OUT

In pairs, act out what you would say if you were:
– the smoker and the non-smoker in (1).
– the two car drivers in (2).
– the manager of the shoe shop and the customer in (8).
– the two friends in (10).

TALKING POINT

If you knew you could devote your life to any single occupation – in music, writing, acting, business, politics, medicine, etc – and be among the best and most successful in the world at it, what would you choose and why?

LISTENING

Listen to some people discussing the same question. Which occupations did they choose? Did they give the same answers as you?

33

Communication

Polite requests for information

🔲 DIALOGUE

EVE: Hello. Can I speak to Dave Edgar please?
WOMAN: I'm afraid he isn't home from work yet. Who's speaking?
EVE: It's Eve Maxwell here, a friend of his. Have you any idea when he'll be back?
WOMAN: I'm not sure. He sometimes works late.
EVE: I see. Could you tell me what his work number is? I'm afraid I've lost it.
WOMAN: Yes, hold on while I look in the book. It's 31556.
EVE: Thanks. By the way, do you know if he received a parcel this morning?
WOMAN: No, I don't. I could go and ask my husband.
EVE: No, don't bother. I'm phoning from a public call box. Anyway, thanks for your help. Goodbye.
WOMAN: Goodbye.

Listen and answer the questions.

1 Who does Eve want to speak to?
2 Where is he?
3 Do you think the woman is Dave Edgar's
   a) wife b) landlady c) girlfriend?
4 What three things does Eve want to know?

FOCUS

- **Asking for information politely:**

  Could/Can you tell me what his work number is, please?
  Have you any idea when he'll be back?
  Do you know if he received a parcel this morning?

  Points to note
  - Polite requests for information are followed by an indirect question in the subordinate clause:
    Could/Can you tell me +what his work number is, please?
    The word order in the subordinate clause is always: subject + verb.

- The subordinate clause can be introduced by a question word, e.g. *what/where/how,* or by *if*:
  Do you know where he is?
  Do you know if he received a parcel this morning?

- If you have several questions to ask the same person, it is perfectly polite to start with an indirect question and continue with direct questions.

UNIT 33: Communication

PRACTICE
Convert the following direct questions into indirect questions.

EXAMPLE
1 How far is it to Avebury?
   Do you know how far it is to Avebury?

2 Is there a hamburger restaurant here?
   Can you tell me . . .
3 Where's the nearest bank?
   Could you tell me . . .
4 What time does the market close?
   Have you any idea . . .
5 Where can I buy a phone card?
   Can you tell me . . .
6 Are there any buses which go from here to the station?
   Could you tell me . . .

ACT IT OUT
In pairs, act out three conversations.

Write down two consecutive questions you might want to ask in each of the following places: 1) a railway station 2) a post-office and 3) a sports stadium.

Then take turns to ask politely for information in each place. Make sure you start the conversation with an indirect question and give sensible replies to each question.

EXAMPLE
A: Excuse me, can you tell me what time the next train to Bath leaves?
B: Yes, it leaves at 10.15.

LISTENING
Before you listen

Adrian Taylor is planning to sail singlehanded across the Atlantic. Think of six questions to ask him.

EXAMPLE
Why do you want to sail the Atlantic alone?

Listen

Note the questions which the interviewer asked Adrian Taylor. How many of the questions were the same as yours? Which of them were indirect questions?

True or false?

1 Adrian is doing the trip because a friend challenged him to do it.
2 He's been training hard.
3 So far he has received £80 in sponsorship.
4 He doesn't know exactly when he is going to leave.
5 He's hoping to complete the trip in less than a month.
6 His family are worried about the trip.

WRITING

Write a short newspaper article about Adrian Taylor and give it a suitable headline.

Start like this:

BON VOYAGE!
On Saturday, 15th June, Adrian Taylor, aged twenty-two, is leaving Portsmouth in an attempt to sail singlehanded across the Atlantic. To prepare for the crossing, Adrian has been . . .

Read about Britain

Find out how to use a phone card.

ABOUT BRITAIN

Phone cards

In many telephone booths in Britain you can use phone cards instead of money. These cards come in 10p units (20, 40, 100 or 200) and are on sale at post offices, newsagents and railway stations. To make a phone call you insert the card, dial the number and speak. As you talk, you can see on the digital display how many units you have left on the card.

-34-

Grammar

Have/get something done

🔊 DIALOGUE

MAN: You need some more brake fluid. That's why the warning light's on.
EVE: I'm having the car serviced on Friday. I'll get the brake fluid topped up then.
MAN: I think you ought to have it done straightaway. I'll do it for you now.
EVE: Fine. By the way, I'd like my tyres checked too, please.
MAN: Sure.

Listen and answer the questions.
1 Why is the warning light on?
2 What's happening on Friday?
3 What else would Eve like done?

What's the difference in meaning?
1 I'm servicing the car.
2 I'm having the car serviced.

FOCUS

Causative 'have' and 'get'

- To *have* or *get something done* means that you arrange for someone else to do a job; you do not do it yourself:
  I'm having/getting the car serviced on Friday.
  I think you ought to have/get it done straightaway.

- *I'd like it done* is a shorter and more usual way of saying: *I'd like to have it done.*

PRACTICE

1 In pairs, say what you are going to have done at the Red Star Garage.

EXAMPLE
I'm going to have my tyres checked.

Then ask for it to be done.

EXAMPLE
I'd like my tyres checked, please.

RED STAR GARAGE
Special Offer This Week!
With every £50 you spend:
FREE
tyres and oil check
car wax and polish
windscreen wash
battery check

UNIT 34: Grammar

2 Define the following people and places.

a decorator   a plumber   a carpenter   a builder   an engineer
a garage   a cleaner   a tailor   a dressmaker

Say which of the following jobs you do yourself and which you have done by the people or the places above.

EXAMPLE
A: Do you do your own decorating?
B: It depends. I do small jobs myself but if it's a big job, I have it done by a painter and decorator.

A: Would you repair a leaking tap yourself?
B: No, I can't do things like that myself. I'd get/have it repaired by a plumber.

Do you . . . ?
1 do your own decorating
2 alter or mend your own clothes
3 service your own car
4 clean your own home

Would you . . . yourself?
5 repair a leaking tap
6 repair/fix your TV
7 make some bookshelves
8 knock down or build a wall

LISTENING
Before you listen

Is it usual to rent televisions in your country? What do you do if the television goes wrong? Why is an aerial necessary on a television set?

Listen

A woman goes into a TV rental shop with a complaint. Note the customer's name, address and complaint and the date and time when the engineer can visit.

READING
Before you read

What do you understand by the following expressions?

put up with   out of order   vandalised

Look at the quotations on the right and read what some Americans have to say about the British telephone system. Note down the three complaints they make. Do you agree?

TALKING POINT

In your country, how easy is it to get your telephone repaired, to get a new telephone installed, or to find a public telephone that works?

WRITING
Linking devices: comparison and contrast

Whereas is used to compare and contrast statements of fact.

EXAMPLE
In New York, you can get a telephone fixed within an hour, *whereas* here in Britain it can take days or weeks.

Choose an aspect of everyday life, e.g. education, entertainment, food, transport etc., and compare what you know of the life in Britain, Australia, Canada or the USA with that of your country. Use *whereas* to introduce the comparisons.

'A New Yorker can get a telephone fixed within the hour, even in the evening, whereas here it can take days or weeks to get your phone repaired. Why do the British put up with this service?'

(Ed Malkovich, journalist with Time-Life.)

'In New York, every telephone on every street corner works. In London it's hard to find a public phone that's not out of order or vandalised.'

(Donna Li, a student at the American College.)

'We applied three months ago to have a new telephone system installed in our office. We're still waiting.'

(Jo-Ann Pepper, PR consultant.)

Reading

Competitive Women

Management Consultant Rennie Fritch says:

'I don't agree with people who say you have to be tougher than the toughest man in order to succeed in business.'

'Instead of trying to be macho, tough and ruthless, women should aim to be strong, resilient and fair. By doing this they can be very competitive.'

Women who try to copy their male colleagues pay a high price, claims Rennie. 'These macho women who try to be copies of men end up sacrificing everything for the company.'

She believes one of the main reasons why women fail to reach the top is their low self-image, a syndrome that starts from an early age. 'Ask a boy, who is expected by his teacher to get sixty per cent in an exam, how he himself expects to do and he will answer confidently that he expects to get seventy or seventy-five per cent,' she says. 'Ask a girl the same question and she will say that she doesn't really expect to pass but she might get fifty per cent.'

Women should be more realistic and objective about themselves. 'Let's face it,' says Rennie, 'if you don't rate yourself highly, how can you expect anyone else to?'

'Women who do make it to the top are always outstanding,' claims Rennie, 'which is not always true of men.'

'When I start meeting women who are not as brilliant as they think they are, I'll know that women have really made it,' she says.

- The competitive woman must pay plenty of attention to her image.
- Never underrate yourself. Men rarely do!
- Believe in yourself, even if others don't.
- Don't worry about making mistakes. You are entitled to make wrong decisions.

Before you read

1 Do you think there are fewer women than men in top jobs? If so, why?

Read the extract above about women in business. Do you agree with Ms Fritch? What does she think is the main reason why women fail to reach the top?

THINK ABOUT IT

1 What do you think Rennie Fritch means by 'macho women' and 'women end up sacrificing everything for the company.'?
2 Does Rennie Fritch have a high opinion of all the men who make it to the top?

🔊 LISTENING

Andrew is talking about business people and their image. Note how he describes the difference between the 'traditional' and the 'modern' image of a businessman

Discuss if you agree with what he says.

VOCABULARY

Match the words below with their dictionary definitions and underline the meaning which is used in the article.

competitive   ruthless   resilient

1 ▇▇▇▇ 1 (of a substance) able to spring back to the former shape or position when pressure is removed: *Rubber is more* ▇▇▇ *than wood.* 2 *apprec* able to return quickly to usual health or good spirits after going through difficulty, disease, change, etc.: *It's been a terrible shock, but she's very* ▇▇▇ *and will get over it soon.* — ~ly *adv* —-ence, -ency *n* [U]:

2 ▇▇▇▇ 1 of, based on, or decided by competition: *the* ▇▇▇ *nature of private industry |* ▇▇▇ *sports* 2 liking to compete: *Jane's got a very* ▇▇▇ *nature.* 3 (of a price, product, or producer) able to compete because it is at least as good, cheap, etc. as the competitors: *I always shop at that supermarket; its prices are very* ▇▇▇ — ~ly *adv* — ~ness *n* [U]

3 ▇▇▇▇ 1 (of a person or their behaviour) showing no human feelings; without pity or forgiveness: *The enemy killed women and children with* ▇▇▇ *cruelty.* 2 not always derog firm in taking unpleasant decisions: *We'll have to be* ▇▇▇ *if we want to eliminate unnecessary waste.* — ~ly *adv* — ~ness *n* [U]

36

Grammar

Past modal verbs: *should have*, and *ought to have*

> We're going to be late. We really should have left earlier.

> Well, you shouldn't have talked so long on the phone.

Look at the picture and answer the questions.

1 Why are the couple upset?
2 Why is it the man's fault?

FOCUS

'Should have'/'ought to have'

- These structures are used to criticise actions in the past i.e., to say that something was wrong or done incorrectly:
  *We should have/ought to have left earlier.
  You shouldn't have/oughtn't to have talked so long on the phone.*

Points to note
- *Ought to* is more emphatic than *should*.
- These structures also have a continuous form:
  You should have been wearing a seatbelt.

PRACTICE

1 Write sentences for the following situations.

EXAMPLE
1 I've been waiting for hours for you to phone!
  You should have/ought to have phoned earlier.

2 I told you not to invite Jack. He's always so boring at parties.
3 Look at the time! It's hours past your bedtime.
4 I'm not surprised Mark is ill. All the ice cream is finished.
5 No wonder they're getting divorced. They were only eighteen when they got married.
6 Oh no! I thought she said everyone was going to wear jeans!

2 Say what the people were doing wrong.

EXAMPLE
1 She was driving so fast that she missed the turning off the motorway.
  She shouldn't have been driving so fast.

2 He fell off his scooter and hurt his head. Of course, he wasn't wearing his helmet!
3 I suppose you were reading without your glasses? No wonder you've got a headache!
4 Of course the park attendant was angry. You weren't supposed to be walking on the grass!
5 He was cycling without lights. That's why a policeman stopped him.

TALKING POINT

In pairs or groups, discuss who was to blame in this situation and why.

When two seventeen-year-old schoolboys walked into a car showroom in Oxford yesterday and asked to test-drive a new Porsche, a salesman gave them the keys. They drove off at high speed and were later involved in an accident on the motorway. Fortunately nobody was hurt, but the Porsche was a write-off.

WRITING

You came to England to support your football team in an international match. Unfortunately at the match there was a serious outbreak of 'football hooliganism'. Write a letter of complaint to a newspaper, using the notes below to criticise the way the event was organised.
– fans allowed to take drink and bottles into the stadium
– no body search or check for weapons
– alcohol on sale inside the stadium
– fans were not separated

Use this guide:
I am writing to complain about the organisation of . . . on . . . . Firstly, . . . /Secondly . . . /Also . . . /And lastly . . . . /It is not surprising that . . . .

Topic 37

Ethics

How far does friendship go?

Ethical choices usually involve love, work, friendship or money – sometimes all four. Occasionally we are faced with a simple decision between good and evil, though usually we find ourselves trying to choose between the lesser of two evils. The distinction between right and wrong is not always clear cut.

David found himself in a personal, professional and ethical dilemma when one of his closest friends learned there was a public relations job coming up in David's company. The friend asked David to recommend him for the job but David didn't think his friend would be able to handle the work.

'I think I could probably help him get the job, but if he weren't my friend I wouldn't recommend him. What if we employed him, at least partly on my say-so, and he was no good? But I really hate to say no to a good friend.'

David made a half-hearted recommendation that revealed his reservations about his friend's capabilities and his friend was satisfied even though he didn't get the job.

But Anne Boe, president of a management consultancy firm, says David handled the situation wrongly. 'I think he should have told his friend the truth – perhaps taken him out to dinner and told him that he wasn't right for the job. I know it's pretty likely that David's friend would be angry with him but there's no easy way out. When you get into a mess of this kind, it's not because you are protecting your friend's feelings but because you're protecting yourself from your friend's anger.'

Glossary
public relations the work of promoting a favourable opinion of an organisation in the mind of the public
say-so (coll) recommendation
management consultancy firm a company which sells advice about management to other organisations

Before you read

Study these words and phrases and say what you think the article on the left will be about.

friend   ask   recommend
job   not able to handle it
dilemma

Words to learn
ethical   handle   half-hearted
reservation   protect

1 Read and answer.

1. How did David's friend want David to help him?
2. Why wasn't David happy about doing this?
3. What ethical choice did David have to make?
4. How did he solve the problem?
5. What should he have done, according to Ann Boe?

2 Read and think.

1. What qualities do you think you need in public relations?
2. How do you think you give a 'half-hearted recommendation'?

3 About you

1. Do you think Anne Boe's criticism was right? Would you tell a friend or close relative the truth if you knew it was going to hurt?
2. Have you ever been asked to lie for a friend? How did it feel? Was it worth it?
3. Do you think 'little white lies' are acceptable?

UNIT 37: Topic

TALKING POINT

In pairs or groups, discuss what you would do in the following situations.

1 You have just had a meal in a restaurant. The food and the service were very poor. When the bill arrives, you notice the waiter has undercharged you by a pound. Would you point out the mistake or pay the bill and leave?

2 A friend gives you some money and asks you to get him/her some duty-free cigarettes when you are next travelling abroad. You disapprove of smoking. Would you say anything or simply get the cigarettes for your friend?

3 Your sister asks you to say she is ill in bed when her boyfriend phones, but you know that she is going out with another boy that evening. Would you lie for her?

4 You see a job advertised which you would very much like to get. The job demands certain qualifications, one of which you do not have. Would you apply, saying that you had all the qualifications?

VOCABULARY

1 Complete the missing verbs and adjectives in the table below.

NOUN	VERB
decision	decide
qualification	
recommendation	
reservation	

NOUN	ADJECTIVE
ability	able
capability	
possibility	
probability	

2 Word stress

Words ending in *ion* are stressed on the syllable before the last.

EXAMPLE
decISion

Words ending in *ity* are stressed on the second to last syllable.

EXAMPLE
aBIlity.

Copy the nouns from the Vocabulary exercise and write the stressed syllables in capital letters. Then listen to the tape and repeat the words to see if you were right.

LISTENING

Before you listen

What does *grant* mean?
What is the difference between an estimate and a bill?

Listen

Dennis, a builder, talks about a recent dilemma. Listen and answer the questions.

1 What did Dennis agree to do?
2 What was the newsagent trying to get from the council?
3 What did the newsagent ask Dennis to do?
4 How did Dennis react?
5 Do you think he did the right thing?

WRITING

Linking devices: contrasting ideas

In formal writing, contrasting ideas can be indicated by *however*.

EXAMPLES
We usually stay at home in the summer. *However,* this year we are going to England.

We usually stay at home in the summer.
This year, *however,* we are going to England.

Notice that *however* can come first in a sentence, or after the word or phrase which it is contrasting.

1 Write pairs of sentences with *however* to express contrast. Use your own ideas.

1 On weekdays . . . at the weekend . . .
2 Now and again . . . most of the time . . .
3 In the past . . . recently . . .
4 I used to think . . .
5 The Mediterranean was once . . .
6 People think that the British . . .
7 Nowadays in the Soviet Union . . .
8 In the USA there are . . .

2 Now write some contrasting sentences about where you live, your job and learning English.

-38-

Communication

Explanation and clarification

🔲 DIALOGUE

Ben is home for the weekend during his last year at college.

MOTHER: What are you doing?
BEN: I'm filling in this application form for a VSO job. I don't know whether to type it or not.
MOTHER: I would. It looks much better if you type it.
BEN: O.K. Listen, it says here that: 'You may add a supporting statement if you wish.' What does 'a supporting statement' mean?
MOTHER: It's something extra you add to an application form. In other words, you get a chance to say something more about yourself.
BEN: I don't understand why they need more information about me when I've put everything on the form.
MOTHER: Well, it's also an opportunity to say why you think you're suitable for the job. When I worked in the personnel department at ICI it was amazing how many people didn't bother to add one to their CV.
BEN: Well, I suppose I'd better write something then. But I don't know what to say.
MOTHER: You can think of something, surely. You must know why you want the job.
BEN: I'm not sure now. I don't know whether I want it or not.
MOTHER: Ben!

Listen and answer the questions.

1 What is Ben doing?
2 What is his first problem?
3 Why is a supporting statement useful?
4 Why doesn't Ben start to write it?

FOCUS

Explanation/clarification

- Asking for and giving explanations:
  What's a CV?
  It's a curriculum vitae.

  What does 'VSO' stand for?
  It stands for 'Voluntary Service Overseas'.

  What does 'a supporting statement' mean?
  It means something you add to an application form.

- Asking indirectly for advice and help:
  I don't know whether to type it or not.
  I don't know what to say.

- Asking indirectly for clarification:
  I don't understand why they need more information.

PRACTICE

1 In pairs, ask for and give explanations of the following abbreviations.

EXAMPLE
A: What does 'i.e.' mean?
B: It means 'that is' or 'that is to say'.
A: What does 'EFL' stand for?
B: It stands for 'English as a Foreign Language'.

i.e.   e.g.   etc.   N.B.   P.S.   R.S.V.P.
EFL   UFO   EEC   BBC   CIA   AIDS

2 In pairs, think of four well-known abbreviations and ask another pair to explain them.

3 Match the expressions below with their correct explanations.

1 out of work	a) to have enough practical knowledge to do something
2 a workaholic	b) work divided into different periods of time
3 to work something out	c) work which is difficult or tiring
4 hard work	d) official permission to work in a country
5 shift work	e) unemployed
6 social work	f) a person who is unable to stop working
7 in working order	g) to find the answer to a problem
8 to have a working knowledge	h) functioning without any problems
9 a work permit	i) work done to help people in poor social conditions

4 Now practise asking for and giving explanations for the expressions in Exercise 3, using the following:

What's . . .? What does . . . mean? Could you tell me/Could you explain what . . . means? It means . . ./I'm afraid I don't know what it means.

5 You are applying for a credit card. You don't understand why certain information is required by the finance company. Use the headings on the form to question the information.

EXAMPLE
I don't understand why they need to know how many children I've got./if I've got any children.

[Credit card application form with fields: Address, Telephone numbers (Home, Business), Married, Single, Widowed, Divorced, No. of children aged 11-18, 3-10, Under 3, Your occupation, Gross income, Monthly income, Residential status, Owner, Tenant]

[Advertisement:
KIDS FAMILY CENTRE
Requires
TEMPORARY PLAY LEADERS
To run our Easter Playscheme
Days are: Tuesday 5 — Friday 8 April
Monday 11 — Friday 15 April
Experience of adventure play and/or special needs necessary.
SALARY: £30.00 PER DAY
Apply to:
THE SECRETARY
KIDS FAMILY CENTRE
60 FLETE SQUARE
LONDON W1
TEL: 01-980 7766

SENIOR FINANCE OFFICER
We are currently looking for men and women to work]

6 Look at the advertisement above. You are interested in the job as Play Leader but you are not sure how to write the letter or what to put in it. Discuss the queries with your partner.

EXAMPLE
A: I don't know how to write the date in English.
B: You write it like this – 16th February.
A: I don't know whether to . . .

1 How do I write the date in English?
2 Do I write my name at the top of the letter or not?
3 Where do I put the name and address of the person I'm writing to?
4 How do I start the letter?
5 How do I end the letter?
6 Do I include a CV or not?

WRITING

Write a letter applying for the job as Play Leader. Say why you think you are suitable for the job. Give details of any relevant experience you have had with children and say when you would be available for interview.

LISTENING

1 Listen to a man enrolling on an English course and note what he says when he asks for information or clarification.
2 Listen again. When you hear 'bleep', ask for the same information, using the language taken from this lesson.

— 39 —

Grammar

Past modal verbs: *could have, might have, must have* and *can't have*

(Speech bubbles from the comic:)
- I wonder what's happened to Laura.
- She could have had a late meeting at the office, I suppose.
- I've just rung Laura at home and her line's engaged. She must have forgotten about this evening.
- She can't have forgotten. I saw her write it in her diary.
- Come on, let's go in. I don't want to miss the beginning.

Answer the questions.

1 Do Laura's friends know why she is late?
2 What does one of the men think has happened?
3 What does the woman think has happened? Why?
4 Why does the man disagree?

FOCUS
'May/might/could/must/can't have'

I He She It We You They	may might could can't must	have	seen it. bought it. done it. finished it.

- **May/might/could have** are used when the speaker is speculating about the past:
  She could have had a late meeting at the office.
  She may/might have got the wrong day.
  These are all similar in meaning.

- **Must have/can't have** are used when the speaker is drawing a conclusion about something that happened in the past:
  She must have forgotten about this evening.
  She can't have forgotten.

Note
These structures also have a continuous form.
She might/must/can't have been waiting all morning.

What's the difference in meaning?

1 He might have left his glasses on the table.
2 He must have left his glasses on the table.
3 He can't have left his glasses on the table.

88

UNIT 39: Grammar

PRACTICE

1 Complete the sentences using *must have* or *can't have* and the verb in brackets.

EXAMPLE
1 She didn't answer the door bell even though I rang several times.
She . . . (be) asleep.
She must have been asleep.

2 I . . . (run out of) petrol. I only filled up the tank this morning.
3 I'm so sorry I'm late. You . . . (wonder) what had happened.
4 Cathy's got a new BMW! She . . . (win) a lottery.
5 I . . . (lose) my glasses. They were here a minute ago.
6 The flowers are beautiful! They . . . (cost) you a fortune.
7 Alan . . . (get lost). I gave him the address and drew a map.

2 Gerry is late for a business meeting. Speculate about what has happened to him using the notes below.

get caught in a traffic jam – watch/stop – car/break down – forget the day – oversleep – have accident

EXAMPLE
He may/might/could have got caught in a traffic jam.

ACT IT OUT

Telephone to find out if Gerry has left home.

GERRY	YOU
Answer the phone.	
	Ask Gerry why he isn't at the meeting.
Apologise and explain that you aren't feeling well.	
	Say what you thought might have happened.
Explain that you were sick all night and that it must have been something you ate.	
	Tell Gerry what you think he should have done.
Apologise and say when you'll be able to get in to work.	

The Salisbury Hotel
Mrs Sheila Nesbitt
Assistant Manager
Salisbury, Wiltshire tel: 0722 3891
Children and dogs welcome.

WRITING

You think you must have left your diary at The Salisbury Hotel when you stayed there recently. You are not sure if you left it in your room or in reception when you were making a phone call. Write a letter to the hotel manager and explain. Lay out your letter formally and include the necessary addresses and today's date. Start your letter *Dear Mrs Nesbitt* and end *Yours sincerely* and your name.

PARAGRAPH 1
Say when you were a guest at the hotel and why you are writing.

PARAGRAPH 2
Describe the diary and any identifying features it has. Give any helpful suggestions as to where and how you might have lost it.

PARAGRAPH 3
Ask the manager to forward the diary if she finds it.

LISTENING

mug² *v* -gg- [T] to rob (a person) with violence, esp. in a public place —**mugging** *n* [C;U]: *a big increase in the number of muggings in this area*

Before you listen

1 Have you ever been mugged or do you know anyone who has?
2 What effect has the incident had on you or the person you know?
3 Find out the meaning of the following words:
attack   vulnerable   assault
bump into   ashamed

Listen

You are going to hear about a mugging incident on Charing Cross Bridge, in London. Make notes under these headings:
Who? When? Where? What? How? What effect?

About the author

Maya Angelou started writing quite late in life. She was forty-one when her first novel: *I Know Why the Caged Bird Sings* was published. She was born in 1928 in St Louis, Missouri. After the break-up of her parents' marriage, she and her brother went to live with their grandmother but later moved to California to live with their mother. At sixteen, Maya gave birth to her son, Guy. In the years that followed, she was a waitress, singer, actress, dancer and black activist as well as a mother. The scene that follows is taken from her second book: *Gather Together in My Name*.

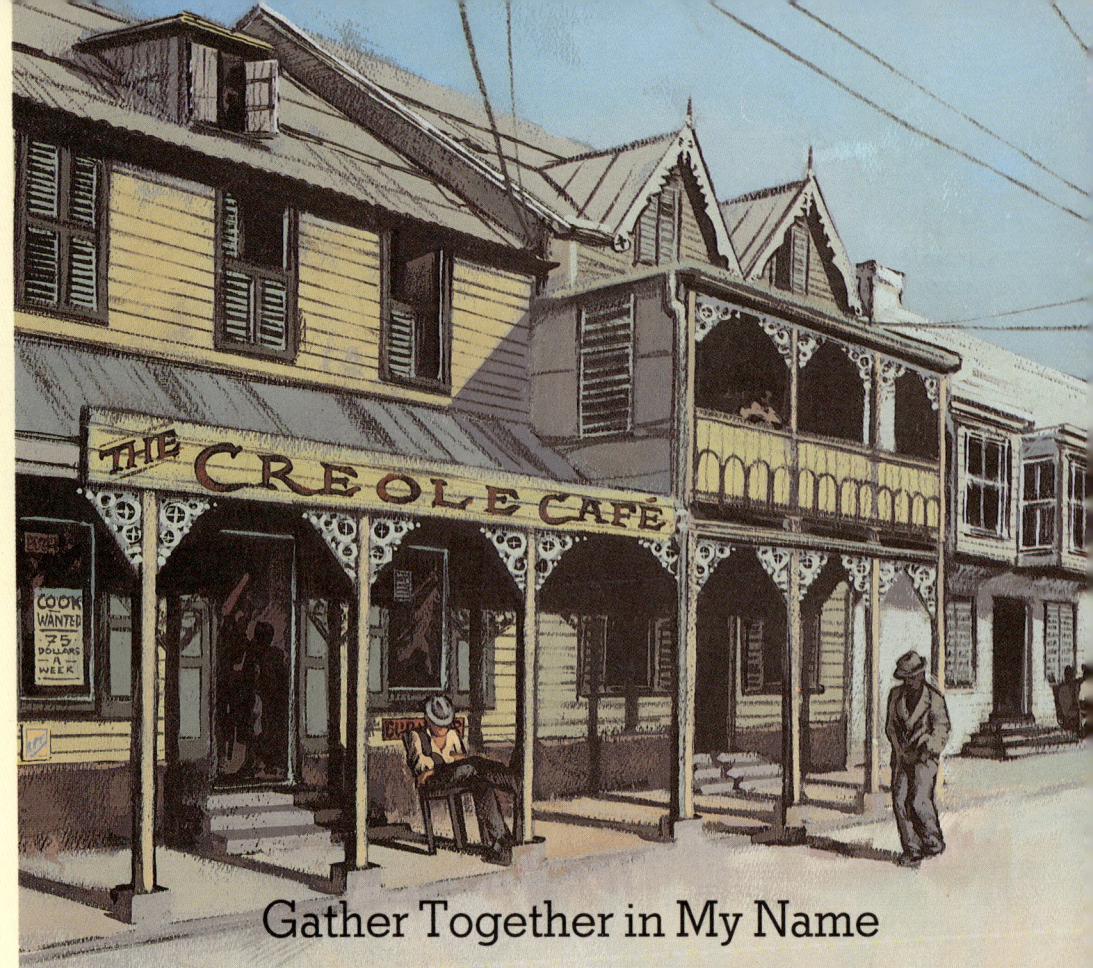

Gather Together in My Name

'Can you cook Creole?'
I looked at the woman and gave her a lie as soft as melting butter.
'Yes, of course. That's all I know how to cook.'
The Creole Café had a cardboard sign in the window which said: *Cook wanted. Seventy-five dollars a week.* As soon as I saw it I knew I could cook Creole, whatever that was.
Desperation to find help must have blinded the woman to my age or perhaps it was the fact that I was nearly six feet and had an attitude which belied my seventeen years. She didn't question me about recipes and menus, but doubt hung on the edge of her questions.
'Can you start on Monday?'
'I'll be glad to.'
'You know it's six days a week. We're closed on Sunday.'
'That's fine with me. I like to go to church on Sunday.'
It's awful to think that the devil gave me that lie, but it came unexpectedly and worked like dollar bills. Suspicion and doubt raced from her face, and she smiled.
'Well, I know we're going to get along. You're a good Christian. I like that. Yes, ma'am, I sure do.'
My need for a job caught and held the denial.

'What time on Monday?'
'You get here at five.'
Five in the morning!
'All right, I'll be here at five, Monday morning.'
Mrs Dupree was a short plump woman of about fifty. Her hair was naturally straight and heavy.
'And what's your name?'
'Rita.' Marguerite was too solemn, and Maya too rich-sounding. 'Rita' sounded like dark flashing eyes, hot peppers and Creole evenings with strummed guitars. 'Rita Johnson.'
'That's a right nice name.' Then, like some people do to show their sense of familiarity, she immediately narrowed the name down.
'I'll call you Reet. Okay?'
Okay, of course. I had a job. Seventy-five dollars a week. So I was Reet. All Reet. Now all I had to do was learn to cook.

Glossary
black activist someone actively fighting for the rights and freedoms of black people
Creole hot, spicy food of French origin typical of the southern USA
belied gave a false idea of

Reading

Guess the meaning

doubt   suspicion   get along   denial
solemn   familiarity

COMPREHENSION

1 Answer the questions.

1 What sort of food did the café specialise in?
2 How much money would Maya get?
3 How many days a week would she work?
4 Did she get the job?
5 What time did she have to get to the café in the morning?
6 Why did she like the name Rita? What was her real name in full?
7 What did Mrs Dupree want to call her?
8 How many lies did Maya tell?

2 Complete the sentences correctly.

1 Maya:
a) knew how to cook Creole food.
b) pretended she knew how to cook Creole food.
c) never cooked anything but Creole food.

2 The woman in the café:
a) knew Maya was seventeen.
b) thought she might be seventeen.
c) thought she was older than seventeen.

3 The woman asked Maya:
a) if she could start on Monday.
b) what recipes she knew.
c) if she was a Christian.

4 Maya:
a) went to church every Sunday.
b) went to church on another day of the week.
c) wasn't a regular churchgoer.

5 The woman was more sure about Maya when Maya told her that she:
a) went to church.
b) didn't mind getting up at five.
c) could cook Creole food.

6 The woman shortened the name Rita to Reet because:
a) she thought Rita sounded too solemn.
b) she thought it was too long.
c) she wanted to sound friendly.

THINK ABOUT IT

1 Would you describe Maya's story as sad, amusing or silly?
2 Do you think Maya's lies were serious?

STYLE
Imaginative description

One way in which writers make their descriptions vivid and exciting is by using similes and metaphors. Remember that a simile compares one thing to another by using *like* or *as*, e.g. *She acted like a maniac. His hands were as cold as ice.*

A metaphor also compares things but doesn't use *like* or *as*. It describes something with words that are usually used to describe something else, e.g. *The sun reached out and stroked my face.*

Reread the text. How does how Maya Angelou express the following ideas?

1 I told a lie smoothly.
2 Her questions contained doubt.
3 Suddenly there was no sign of doubt or suspicion on her face.
4 I so badly needed a job that I didn't deny that I was a Christian.
5 Rita was an exciting-sounding name.

TALKING POINT

What problems do you think Maya Angelou might have had as a black, unmarried mother living in San Francisco in the early 1940s?

WRITING

Look at the text about the author, Maya Angelou, then use the following notes to write a short biography about Carson McCullers, a white woman who wrote about the 'Deep South' of the USA.

```
Carson McCullers
American writer (1917-67)

- first book/aged 23/'The Heart
  is a Lonely Hunter' (1940)

- born Columbus, Georgia/
  originally wanted to be a musician

- married at 20/difficult marriage/ended
  in husband's suicide 1953

- established reputation as a writer with
  'Reflections in a Golden Eye' (1941),
  and 'Member of the Wedding' (1946)

- in spite of ill-health and alcoholism,
  wrote until her death in 1967
```

Self check 4

Units 31–40

1 Match the two halves of the sentences.

1 If I were you,
2 If they knew where she was,
3 I wouldn't take the job,
4 Would you go to China,
5 If you left at five,
6 What would you do with the money,

a) if they offered you a job there?
b) you'd get there by six.
c) they wouldn't worry so much.
d) if you won?
e) I'd get a new one.
f) if I were you.

2 Write the correct form of the verbs in brackets.

1 If you (not know) he was English, you would never guess.
2 If you found £10 in the street, (you/give) it to the police?
3 I (not/wear) jeans if I were you.
4 You (get) there on time if you took the five o'clock train.
5 If I (have) a rest now, I'd fall asleep.
6 A: (you/marry) him if he asked you?
   B: No, I (not/marry) him if he (be) the last man on earth!

3 Complete the second half of the sentences.

1 You'll break it if (you/be/not) careful.
2 I wouldn't go unless (I/have to).
3 If you drink that water (you/be) ill.
4 Would you feel better if (she/apologise)?
5 The cat won't eat the fish unless (you/cook) it.
6 What would you say if (I/phone) the police?

4 Rewrite the questions starting with the phrases provided.

1 Where's John?
  Have you any idea . . .
2 How do I get to the station from here?
  Could you tell me . . .
3 When does the next programme start?
  Can you tell me . . .
4 Have we got any homework?
  Do you know . . .
5 What time does the last underground train leave?
  Have you any idea . . .
6 Did Sam paint that picture?
  Do you know . . .
7 Why is everyone laughing?
  Could you tell me . . .
8 Where is the nearest public phone box?
  Can you tell me . . .

5 Choose the right verb below to write short sentences using *I'd like* and the cues provided.

take away   clean   repair   service   type   cut

EXAMPLE
1 I'd like my car serviced, please.

1 my car   3 my hair   5 this leather jacket
2 this watch   4 these letters   6 all that rubbish

6 Choose the best answer.

1 I'd like to book an appointment to:
  a) have my hair cut.
  b) cut my hair.
  c) have cut my hair.

2 I'll:
  a) have someone to fix it immediately.
  b) get fixed immediately.
  c) have it fixed immediately.

3 I'd like this £5 note:
  a) to have it changed, please.
  b) changing, please.
  c) changed, please.

Self check 4

7 Choose the correct verb form in these sentences.

1 You *should see/should have seen* his face when I told him!
2 When you visit Florence, *you ought to go/ought to have gone* to see the Uffizi gallery.
3 You *shouldn't have taken/shouldn't take* my camera on holiday with you. I was very angry.
4 It's a pity we didn't ask Kelly. We *should think/should have thought* of it earlier.
5 You *ought to write/ought to have written* a book about it soon.

8 Rewrite the following sentences using *should have* or *shouldn't have* and the past participle of the verb.

1 It was wrong of you to keep the change. (You . . .)
2 I'm sorry I got so angry. (I . . .)
3 How stupid of them not to check the time of the train. (They . . .)
4 Why didn't I take my swimming things? (I . . .)
5 The accident was his fault. He was drinking and driving. (He . . .)

9 Complete the sentences using *might have, must have* or *can't have*, and the correct form of the verb in brackets.

1 I can't find my keys anywhere. I think I . . . (lose) them.
2 You shouldn't have driven when it was so foggy. You . . . (have) an accident.
3 You never know. They . . . (take) the wrong bus.
4 She . . . (telephone) because I was in all day.
5 I'm glad you didn't come to see me yesterday. You . . . (catch) my cold.
6 I . . . (lose) my passport. It was here on the table just a few minutes ago.

10 Choose the best answer.

1 TEACHER: Today we are going to read about Mary, who's a physiotherapist.
 STUDENT: Excuse me, but
 a) what means 'physiotherapist'?
 b) can you tell me what 'physiotherapist' means, please?
 c) could you tell me what does 'physiotherapist' mean?

2 TEACHER: What's the matter, Louis? Why aren't you writing anything?
 STUDENT: I don't know
 a) what should I write?
 b) what I am writing.
 c) what to write.

3 STUDENT: But I don't understand
 a) why you can't use the present tense.
 b) why can't you use the present tense.
 c) why it's not possible the present tense.

11 What would you say in the following situations?

1 You are at a railway station and want to know which platform the train for Bristol leaves from. You ask a porter.
2 You have torn your best suede jacket. You have seen a notice at the dry cleaner's saying: 'We do alterations and repairs' so you take your jacket along.
3 A travel agent advises you to buy an Apex ticket. You have never heard of this type of ticket before and ask for an explanation.
4 A teacher is leaving at the end of term and you have been asked to give a short speech at her leaving party. You go to a friend for help.
5 You have offered to walk home with a friend after a party but your friend wants to walk home alone. You are puzzled.

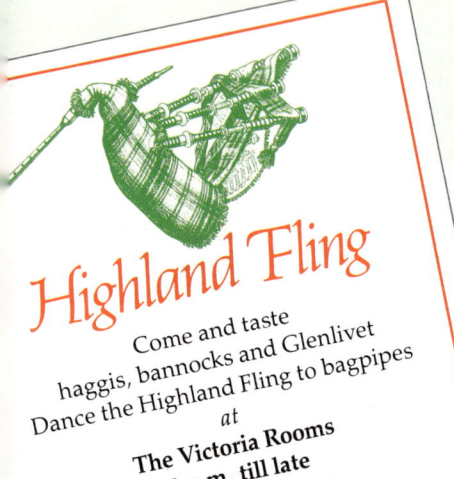

Fluency 4

International food festival

1 Write labels

In pairs, choose two national or regional dishes, one savoury and one sweet, which would best represent your country in the Marlborough International Food Festival. Make labels to accompany each dish. Put your name on one of them and complete the information:

Participant's name: . . .
Name of dish: . . .
Type of dish: . . . (i.e. savoury or sweet)
Country (and region): . . .

2 An explanation

All the labels go into a hat. Each member of the class picks out a label and asks the person whose label it is to explain and describe the dish.

3 A correction game

In groups, ask each person in turn to explain how to prepare their particular dish. Anyone who thinks the speaker has made a mistake must stop the speaker and say: *That's wrong. You said . . . but you should have said . . . .* Keep a score of the mistakes. The winner is the person who is stopped the fewest times.

4 Request for service

You have just arrived at your hotel. It is seven o'clock in the evening. When you open your suitcase you discover that a bottle of lotion has leaked all over the clothes which you want to wear that evening. Phone the hotel housekeeper to explain the problem. Say how you think the accident must have happened and ask for help. Work in pairs. The housekeeper must use the information on the left.

5 Request for information

At the festival you hear about a Scottish evening which sounds interesting. You ask an organiser for more information about the event: when and where it is and what is going to happen. Act out the conversation. The organiser must use the invitation on the left to tell you about the evening and what you will be able to eat, drink and do there.

6 A letter

Write a letter to an English-speaking penfriend about your visit to the International Food Festival in Marlborough. Describe the Scottish evening and say what it was like. Mention the accident you had with your clothes and what you did about it.

MARLBOROUGH INTERNATIONAL FOOD FESTIVAL
Food from 49 countries

Highland Fling

Come and taste haggis, bannocks and Glenlivet
Dance the Highland Fling to bagpipes

at
The Victoria Rooms
8 p.m. till late
Tuesday 29th June

Tickets free from the Scottish Stand in the Main Hall

Glossary
haggis a savoury food like a big sausage made from the heart and other organs of a sheep
bannock a flat cake made of oatmeal
Glenlivet a pure malt scotch whisky
Highland Fling a Scottish country dance that is fast and full of movement

---

Travel Lodge
Housekeeping Service
Dial 08 for the Housekeeper
24-hour service
Laundry, pressing and dry cleaning
Same day service (before 6 p.m.)

Introducing Errol

Look at the pictures of Errol.
What's his job?
What duties does it involve?
What sort of hours do you think he works?
What do you think he likes doing in his free time?
Is he married or single?

Now read about Errol. Were you right?

−41−
Errol

A police officer

SO YOU WANT TO JOIN THE POLICE?

Fay Rowan interviews Errol Mason, a young police officer from Bristol.

WHEN I CONTACTED Police Constable Errol Mason, he was just finishing a nine-day night shift and was understandably trying to catch up on lost sleep. 'It's hard to sleep during the day but you just have to try,' said Errol, 'otherwise you end up exhausted.'

I asked him when we could meet for a chat. 'What about coming along to the ice rink on Tuesday evening — say, about eight?' he suggested. Errol told me that he spent most of his free time playing ice hockey. So the following Tuesday evening I sat and watched Errol skating across the ice. Later, over a cup of coffee, I asked him what his job in the police involved.

'Many people have only one image of the police. They think we spend our time chasing criminals in fast cars with wailing sirens and flashing lights,' said Errol with a grin. 'In fact, that's only one small part of the job. A lot of police work can be quite boring. You can be on the desk doing routine office work for a whole month at a time. Then the next month you may be driving around on patrol. Then, perhaps you're "on the beat" for a bit.'

Errol told me that one of the most interesting parts of the job was in fact 'community policing'. I asked him what this involved. 'You have your own special area which you have to patrol. It really means being on the beat: walking round keeping your eyes open, making sure you know what's going on, chatting to people, basically trying to prevent crime.'

Thinking of some of the recent ugly scenes at football matches and demonstrations, I asked Errol if he was conscious of the dangers involved and if he was ever frightened. 'Sometimes, yes,' he replied. 'Anyone would be. It's just one of the things you learn to accept. Violence is always frightening and a lot more people nowadays are carrying weapons — knives, coshes and so on. Except in extreme circumstances, all we carry are truncheons, handcuffs and a radio.' When I asked if the irregular hours of police work affected his social life, Errol smiled. 'My girlfriend gets a bit annoyed — she says I'm either on night shift or I'm playing ice hockey! But it's not like being a doctor. When you're off duty, that's it. It has to be a real emergency like a major riot or something to be called out on your night off.'

If you think police work sounds like the job for you, write for more information.

Glossary
cosh a short solid rubber or metal tube used as a weapon
truncheon a short stick carried as a weapon by the police
handcuffs a pair of metal rings joined by a short chain for holding together the wrists of a prisoner

UNIT 41: Errol

Words to learn
exhausted   chase   criminal (n)   grin (n)
patrol (n)   demonstration   off duty
emergency   riot

1 Read and find out:
1 where and when the interviewer met Errol.
2 what people think the police spend most of their time doing.
3 what equipment Errol carries.

2 Choose the right answer.
1 According to Errol the best part of his job is:
a) working on night shift.
b) driving around in fast cars.
c) doing 'community policing.'

2 He thinks his job is:
a) more ordinary than people imagine.
b) more exciting than people imagine.
c) easier than people imagine.

3 He says that police work is more dangerous nowadays because:
a) there are so many more football matches and demonstrations.
b) more people are carrying dangerous weapons.
c) the police only carry a truncheon and handcuffs.

4 Errol's girlfriend is annoyed because:
a) he doesn't spend enough time with her.
b) he's always being called out when he's off duty.
c) he never gets any time off.

3 Read and think.
1 Why is working a nightshift more tiring than working a dayshift?
2 How do you think people get their image of the police?
3 Why do you think Errol finds going on the beat interesting?
4 Why do you think the police carry radios?
5 What do you think is an example of 'an extreme circumstance'?

4 About you
1 Have you ever had to report an incident to the police?
2 Do you know any police officers personally? What are they like when they're off duty?

VOCABULARY
1 In what ways are the following crimes similar? What do they each involve?
burglary   shoplifting   robbery
pickpocketing   mugging

2 Complete the list.

PERSON	CRIME	PERSON	CRIME
burglar	burglary	...	shoplifting
...	crime	...	smuggling
...	theft	...	murder
...	robbery	...	pickpocketing
...	rape	...	drug dealing

3 🔊 Listen to the following compound nouns. Copy them, writing the stressed syllables in capital letters.

police officer   police station
drug smuggling   armed robbery
community policing   criminal investigation

EXAMPLE
poLICE   OFFicer

TALKING POINT
1 What aspects of police work do you think are dangerous or unpleasant?
2 Do you think the police treat all sections of society in the same way?
3 What is the public image of the police in your country? Is it accurate?

🔊 LISTENING
Listen to a police officer talking about her work. How does she describe the shift system? What does she think is the most unpleasant part of her job? Why?

– 42 –

Grammar

Reported speech (1)

Look at the sentences.

1 'I spend most of my free time playing ice hockey,' he said.
2 He said that he spent most of his free time playing ice hockey.

Which sentence is in direct speech and which is in reported speech? What happens to the tense of the verb *spend* in reported speech? What other differences are there between the two sentences? Find examples of reported speech in the text about Errol. Which are reported statements and which are reported questions? Check with the Focus section below.

Reported statements

DIRECT STATEMENT	REPORTED STATEMENT
'I'm a police officer.'	He said/told me (that) he was a police officer.
'I live in Bristol.'	He said/told me (that) he lived in Bristol.

Reported questions

DIRECT QUESTION	REPORTED QUESTION
'When can we meet?'	I asked (him) when we could meet.
'Are you ever frightened?'	She asked if he was ever frightened.

FOCUS

- Reported speech is often introduced by *say* and *tell*.
- *Tell* is always followed by a name or an object pronoun:
  He told me he was a police officer.
- When the reporting verb is in the present tense, there is no change in the tense:
  'I don't want to come.'
  He says he doesn't want to come.
- *That* is always optional after verbs of speaking.
- In reported questions the word order of the original question is changed:
  'What's your name?'
  She asked what my name was.

Verb changes

am/is – was
are – were
am/is going to – was going to
have/has – had
go – went
went – had gone
have gone – had gone
can – could
will – would
shall – should
may – might
must – had to

The tense of the verb in the direct speech usually 'moves' further back into the past.

Other changes

today	that day
tonight	that night
tomorrow	the next day
yesterday	the day before
ago	before
last week	the week before
next week	the following week
this/that	the
this morning	that morning
here	there

UNIT 42: Grammar

> I spend most of my free time playing ice hockey.

3 Errol is on duty at the police station. Read or listen to the dialogue and find out what the man has lost, where and when.

DIALOGUE

MAN: I've lost my briefcase. Has one been handed in this morning?
ERROL: No, sir, it hasn't. Where did you lose it?
MAN: Outside my house in Chester Street this morning. I put it on the pavement, then I drove away and forgot about it.
ERROL: Can you describe the briefcase, sir?
MAN: Yes, it's black leather with a combination lock and it has my initials D.B. on it.
ERROL: Is there anything valuable inside it?
MAN: No, there isn't. Just a few papers and some computer discs.
ERROL: Well, we'll let you know if we hear anything about it. Can I have your name and phone number please?

4 Work in pairs. In turn, report the conversation between the man and Errol using reported questions and statements.

A: A man came in and said he had lost . . . He asked if . . .
B: Errol asked him where . . .

PRACTICE

1 Rewrite the following statements in reported speech.

EXAMPLE
1 'I'm going to watch television,' he said to his mother.
   He told his mother (that) he was going to watch television.

2 'We moved to Bristol three years ago,' said the woman.
   She said . . .
3 'I'll come at eight tomorrow,' she said.
   She told me . . .
4 'I've bought a new car,' she said.
   She said . . .
5 'I can't think of anything to write,' said the boy to his teacher.
   The boy told . . .
6 'We're driving the car to France next summer,' they said.
   They said . . .
7 'I must get some new glasses,' he said.
   He said that . . .
8 'I may sell my bicycle,' she said.
   She said . . .

2 Answer these questions about Errol using reported speech in the past. What did Errol say about:

1 sleeping after a night-shift?
2 community policing?
3 the equipment he carries?

WRITING

Complete Errol's report about the missing briefcase.

LOST PROPERTY REPORT
Time: 10 a.m. Date: Monday, 13th June . . .
Item missing: one briefcase with personal contents

At approximately 10 a.m. this morning Mr D. Barton reported the loss of a briefcase . . . . .
Mr Barton said he . . . . .

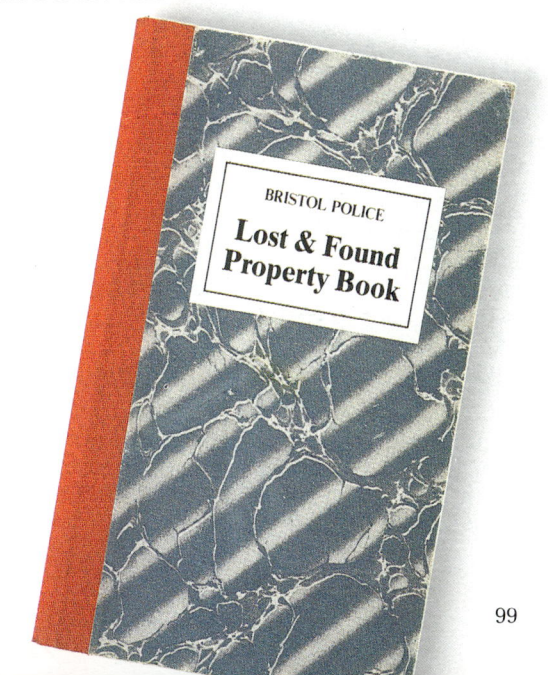

BRISTOL POLICE
Lost & Found Property Book

—43—

Communication

Closing strategies

🔊 DIALOGUE 1 In the office

RAJ: Anyway, it was a very good party.
ANDY: So it seems!
RAJ: Well, I suppose I ought to get on. I've got some work to do.
ANDY: Yes, I must get back to work too.
RAJ: Look, I'll give you a ring about those tickets, O.K?
ANDY: Fine. By the way, good luck with the interview on Monday.
RAJ: Thanks. I'll need it. Bye now.
ANDY: Bye. See you.

🔊 DIALOGUE 2 In a supermarket

TIM: And Helen's starting playschool in the autumn.
JILL: Goodness, doesn't time fly! It seems only yesterday that we were at her christening. Listen, I really ought to be going now. It's getting late and I've got a lot more shopping to do.
TIM: Me too. Look, we must get together, all four of us. Have a meal or something.
JILL: Yes, good idea. Give me a ring some time.
TIM: O.K., I'll do that. Take care and have a good weekend.
JILL: Yes, same to you. Bye!

Read or listen to the dialogues and find out:

1 how the different people signal that they want to end the conversation and what reasons they give.
2 how the other person responds in each case.
3 what arrangements they make for further contact.
4 what leave-taking phrases are used.

FOCUS

Closing strategies

- Ending conversations:
  Well, I suppose I ought to get on.
  Listen, I really have to/ought to be going now.

- Giving a reason for ending the conversation:
  I must get back to work.
  I've got some work to do.
  It's getting late.

- Making arrangements to make contact again:
  (Look), we must get together some time.
  (Listen), why don't we meet for lunch?
  (Look), I'll give you a ring.

- Leave-taking phrases:
  See you (soon/next . . .)
  Good luck with/on . . .
  Give my regards to . . .
  Have a good evening/weekend/time on Monday.
  Take care.
  Bye (for) now.

UNIT 43: Communication

PRACTICE

1 Match the leave-taking phrases with an appropriate response.

1 See you soon.
2 Good luck with the exam.
3 Look, I really must be going.
4 Give my regards to Ann.
5 Have a good holiday!
6 Bye for now.
7 Take care.

a) Yes, and give mine to Pat.
b) I will. Don't worry.
c) Thanks. I'll need it.
d) Yes, see you.
e) Yes, bye.
f) Yes, I must go too.
g) Thanks and the same to you.

2 In pairs, practise ending conversations.

Signal that you want to end the conversation. Give a reason. Make arrangements to make contact some other time, and take your leave.

REASONS FOR ENDING A CONVERSATION:
It's getting late.
You think there's someone at the door.
Someone's coming to see you in a minute.
You've got some work to do.
You've got to telephone someone else.
Someone else wants to use the phone.

EXAMPLE
A: Well, I suppose I ought to get on. It's getting late.
B: Yes, I must get on too.
A: Look, we must get together some time.
B: Yes, why don't we meet for lunch?
A: O.K. I'll give you a ring. Bye for now.
B: Yes, bye.

LISTENING
Before you listen

Look up the meaning of these expressions in your dictionary.

dash   be off   call it a day   cover   wrap up

Listen

You are going to hear endings from four conversations. Listen and note down how the speakers signal the ending of each conversation. Listen again and note what reason they give, if any.

ACT IT OUT

Act out a telephone conversation with a friend who has been ill. Telephone your friend to tell her/him about a party you have been to. Say what it was like and if you enjoyed it.

One of you must end the conversation. Say you have to go and give a reason. Your friend must respond appropriately and make arrangements to meet at another time.

WRITING
Ending informal letters

Well, I must stop now and catch the post.
Well, I think that's all the news.
I'll stop now as it's getting late.

Closing phrases

Look after yourself.
Give my love/regards to . . .
With best wishes, . . .
Write soon.
All my love, . . ./Love, . . .

Use the following guide to write a letter to a friend.

PARAGRAPH 1
Thank your friend for a recent letter and apologise for not writing earlier. Explain why you have been busy.

PARAGRAPH 2
Tell your friend if you are enjoying your English classes or not, and say which lessons you have enjoyed most. Report any special news.

PARAGRAPH 3
Ask your friend for news about home, holidays and family.

PARAGRAPH 4
Give a reason for ending your letter and send regards to any people who know you. Ask your friend to write back as soon as possible.

'Sorry this is so short but I must catch the post!'

-44-

Grammar

Reported speech (2)

Do you fancy a coffee?

When I met Errol at the ice rink, he offered me a coffee.

How many different ways can you offer someone a cup of coffee in English?

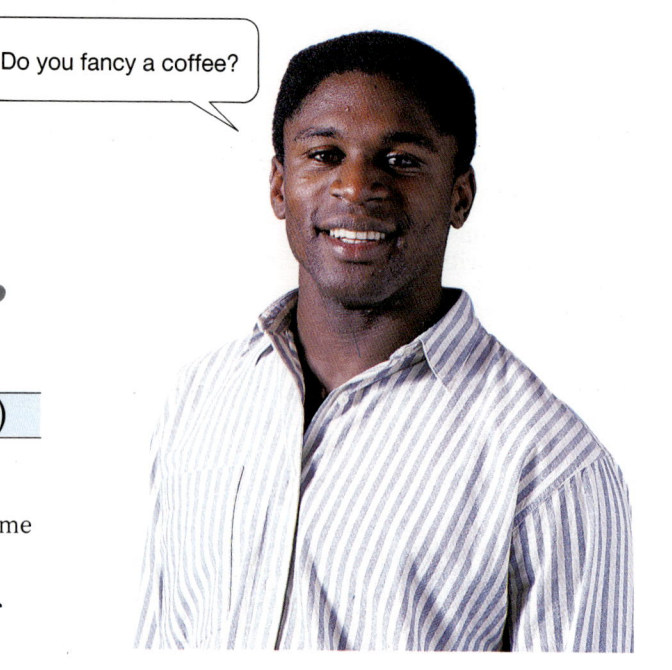

FOCUS

Verbs of reporting

Apart from *say, tell* and *ask*, there are many other verbs which report speech. Here are some of them with the structures which follow them:

- **Verb + object + infinitive**
  advise   remind
  ask   tell
  persuade warn
  He advised me to leave at once.
  He warned me not to stay.

- **Verb + two objects**
  introduce   offer
  She introduced her husband to me.
  He offered me a coffee.

- **Verb + infinitive**
  agree   refuse   promise
  They agreed to come.

- **Verb + that + clause**
  say   explain
  I explained that I wasn't feeling well.

- **Verb + *ing* form**
  suggest
  He suggested meeting at the rink.

- **Verb + preposition + *ing* form**
  apologise
  He apologised for being rude.

- **Verb + object**
  accept   refuse
  I accepted the invitation.

PRACTICE

1 Match the reported speech with the actual words spoken.

REPORTED SPEECH
1 She advised him to get a summer job.
2 She warned him not to drive too fast.
3 He reminded her not to drive too fast.
4 She persuaded her to come.
5 He told them not to be late.
6 She suggested going for a coffee.
7 I offered to help them.
8 He refused to help them.
9 I invited her to lunch.
10 She apologised for being late.
11 She agreed to ask him.
12 He introduced Mary to his colleague.

WORDS SPOKEN
a) 'Mary, meet my friend, Gill.'
b) 'Would you like me to help you?'
c) 'I'm sorry I'm late.'
d) 'If I were you, I'd get a summer job.'
e) 'O.K., I'll ask him.'
f) 'Don't drive too fast. This road is dangerous.'
g) A: Oh, please come! B: Oh, all right then.
h) 'Don't be late!'
i) 'Why don't we go for a coffee?'
j) 'I'm not going to help you.'
k) 'Would you like to come to lunch?'
l) 'Don't forget there's a speed limit here.'

UNIT 44: Grammar

2 Read the following dialogues and choose the verb which best describes the actual words spoken.

1 MIKE: Would you like to come with Greg and me to the open-air concert on Saturday?
   a) apologise   b) offer   c) invite

   JANE: Brilliant! I'd love to come.
   a) accept   b) refuse   c) remind

2 BEN: What should I do about my briefcase?
   a) agree   b) ask   c) introduce

   SUE: Why don't you go to the police station and report it?
   a) offer   b) tell   c) suggest

3 MARK: Mum, please can we go to the carnival? We'll be all right! You know we will!
   a) try to persuade   b) try to agree   c) warn

   MUM: O.K., but don't take a lot of money in case there are pickpockets around.
   a) agree but remind   b) agree but warn   c) refuse

3 Report the conversations using the correct verb of reported speech.

EXAMPLE
Mike invited Jane to a concert, and she . . .

LISTENING

Before you listen

If people who have young children want to go out, what arrangements can they make?

Listen

1 Two people are talking about a broken arrangement.

Note:
what Alan was going to do.
where Paul and his wife were going.
what time Alan arrived.
what excuse Alan made.
what Paul did when Alan finally arrived.

2 Listen again and note the verbs of reporting in the order in which they occur.

WRITING

Write a paragraph from Paul's letter to a friend reporting how Alan let him down the other evening. Use the verbs of reporting that you listed in the Listening exercise.

Start like this:

I'm writing this in a very bad mood. You remember Alan? Well, he really let us down the other evening. We had tickets for . . .

ACT IT OUT

In pairs, use the information above to act out a conversation about a visit to a nightclub.

A
You want to go to a fashionable new nightclub which has opened in a run-down part of the city. You want B to go with you to try it out. Explain that the area isn't really dangerous but suggest going to the club by taxi. Try to persuade your friend to go with you as you do not want to go alone.

B
You have heard about the new nightclub but are not keen to go there because a friend of yours was mugged in that part of the city a few weeks ago and you don't want to go anywhere near it. Besides, you have to start work early in the morning. Agree or refuse to go as you wish.

Reading

The changing role of the police

COMPREHENSION

1 Match the headlines with the correct newspaper article.

1 POLICE HALT NURSES' MARCH
2 POLICE WARNING TO ARMED GANGS
3 POLICE HOLD 18 FOOTBALL FANS IN DAWN RAIDS

A POLICE investigating football violence arrested eighteen people yesterday in dawn raids on homes in London and the Home Counties.

Detectives said they hoped they had 'broken the the back of a hard-core element' of violent football fans. Weapons including knives, coshes and a crossbow were seized by the ninety officers involved in the raids.

B PROTESTING nurses mounted a mass demonstration at the House of Commons yesterday but were held back by a cordon of police, who used five riot control vans to stop the marchers entering Parliament Square.

Some nurses complained of rough treatment by the police. One male nurse claimed he had been hit on the shoulder with a truncheon and at least two nurses were arrested.

C POLICE will use guns and appropriate force when dealing with armed criminals, Scotland Yard warned yesterday. The statement came after a judge sentenced a gang of five to a total of fifty-five years jail for armed robbery.

'When faced with armed criminals, we will reply with appropriate force. Our duty remains to combat crime.'

Glossary
sentence (v) to give official punishment
raid (n) here, a sudden visit by the police looking for criminals or illegal goods
hard core element here, a violent group
crossbow a powerful weapon which combines a bow and a gun

VOCABULARY
Prepositions after verbs

Complete the sentences below with the correct preposition.

for   of   to   with   about   from

EXAMPLE
1 The police often have to deal . . . dangerous criminals.
The police often have to deal with dangerous criminals.

2 The protesters were prevented . . . entering Parliament Square.
3 The children were warned . . . the dangers of drugs.
4 The criminal was sentenced . . . five years in prison.
5 She was accused . . . armed robbery.
6 The nurses complained . . . unnecessary police violence.
7 The demonstrators were arrested outside the South African embassy . . . disturbing the peace.
8 Even on the beat, a police officer might be faced . . . a dangerous situation.

🎧 LISTENING

1 Listen to a radio news report and note:
what London Regional Transport are worried about.
who is causing the trouble.

2 Listen again and note five measures which are being taken to try to solve the problem.

TALKING POINT

1 Should police be present at political demonstrations and sports events like football matches? Should they be armed?
2 Do violent TV programmes and films make police work more dangerous?

-46-

Grammar

Past perfect simple

Errol and his girlfriend, Judy, were very excited because Judy's father had managed to get them two tickets for the football Cup Final at Wembley Stadium. They caught an early train to London and spent the morning looking round the shops. They arrived at Wembley at two o'clock and joined the queue to get in. Imagine their horror at the turnstile when they realised they had left the tickets at home!

Put the events in the order in which they actually occurred.

1 Errol and Judy arrived at Wembley Stadium.
2 They left the tickets at home.
3 They spent the morning shopping.
4 Judy's father gave Errol and Judy two tickets for the Cup Final at Wembley.
5 They caught an early train to London.

What's the difference in meaning?

1 Errol was feeling pleased. He bought himself a new jacket.
2 Errol was feeling pleased. He had bought himself a new jacket.

Look at the Focus section and see if you can find the answer.

FOCUS

The past perfect

This tense is used

- To refer to something that happened before another action or state in the past:
  They were excited because Judy's father had managed to get them tickets for the match.

- To describe earlier events when telling a story in the past:
  What an awful day! Everything had gone wrong from the moment she woke up...

- In reported speech and thoughts:
  They realised they had forgotten the tickets.

PRACTICE

1 Join the sentences using *because* and the past perfect.

EXAMPLE
1 Judy and Errol spent the morning shopping. They were tired.
  Judy and Errol were tired because they had spent the morning shopping.

2 He didn't work hard enough during the year. He failed his exam.
3 Mike left his wallet at home. He was cross.
4 They didn't pay their telephone bill. The telephone company cut them off.
5 They left their passports at home. They couldn't cross the frontier.
6 She lost her glasses. She couldn't read the sign.

2 Complete the following sentences using the past perfect.

1 When I went to pay, I realised that . . .
2 When he arrived at the station, he saw that . . .
3 When they got home, they found that . . .
4 Soon after the wedding, she knew that . . .
5 When I asked about the mess on the floor, she said that . . .

LISTENING

Listen to Errol's young brother, Michael, talking to a friend about something which happened to him recently.
1 Where was Michael going and why?
2 Why did he miss the ferry?

WRITING

Write Michael's story using the notes below to help you. Use the past perfect tense where necessary.

Michael/very excited/got job for skiing season in a resort in Austria. Good skier/skiied a lot at school. Went by train to Dover/and because arrived early/went to a café to get something to drink. Put backpack beside chair/while drinking tea. When went to catch midnight ferry/no ticket or passport/realised someone stolen them.

THE MYSTERY OF AGATHA CHRISTIE.

Agatha Christie (1891-1976) is one of the world's best-known and best-loved authors. Her famous detectives, Hercule Poirot and Miss Marple, and her brilliantly constructed plots have caught the imagination of generations of readers. Although she lived to an old age and wrote many books, she did not reveal much about her personal life.

In December 1926 an incident occurred which would have made an enthralling detective story in itself. At the height of her success with her first novel, she apparently vanished into thin air for ten days. At the time she was extremely distressed because she had found out that her husband was having an affair with another woman and wanted a divorce. She was sleeping badly, she couldn't write and she was eating very little.

On Friday 3rd December, Agatha told her secretary and companion, Carlo (Miss Charlotte Fisher), that she wanted a day alone. When Carlo returned in the evening, she found that the garage doors had been left open and the maids were looking frightened. According to them, Mrs Christie had come downstairs at about eleven in the evening, had got into her car and had driven off quickly without saying anything to anybody.

Carlo waited up anxiously all night but Agatha did not return. Early the next morning the police found Agatha's car in a ditch with its lights on. There was no trace of Agatha.

A nation-wide hunt for the missing novelist was started. The police were suspicious. Did the servants know something more? Was Agatha's husband hiding something? Newspapers printed wild stories about her disappearance — that she had committed suicide, that she had been kidnapped, that she had run away with a secret lover; some even suggested that she had planned the whole thing as a publicity stunt.

The mystery ended ten days later when Agatha was found alive and well in Harrogate, a health spa in Yorkshire. Her husband explained to the waiting reporters that she had lost her memory. But to this day, nobody really knows what happened during those missing ten days.

Glossary
publicity stunt an action to gain attention
health spa a resort with spring water where people come for health cures

47

Topic

Mysteries and thrillers

1 Read and answer.

1. When did Agatha disappear?
2. Why was she distressed at the time?
3. What did she tell her companion, Carlo?
4. What did Carlo find on her return?
5. What had happened at eleven o'clock according to the maids?
6. What did the police find?
7. What did the newspapers suggest had happened to Agatha?
8. Where and when did Agatha reappear?
9. What explanation did her husband give?

2 Guess the meaning

enthralling   vanished into thin air
distressed   ditch   trace   kidnap

3 Cover the text and use the questions and answers from Exercise 1 to retell the story of Agatha Christie's disappearance.

4 Read and think.

1. Do you think Agatha lost her memory?
2. What do you think happened during those ten days?
3. What effect do you think her disappearance had on her marriage after her return?

VOCABULARY

Match the type of book with a suitable title.

BOOK
  a detective story —
  a biography 3
  an autobiography 2
  a thriller —
  a travel book 1
  a romantic novel —
  a collection of short stories 4

  TITLE
  Long Lost Love
  Fear Strikes at Midnight
  'Tramp' and other stories
  The life of Jane Austen
  Mainly Me, Myself and I
  Mystery at Highview House
  In the steps of Marco Polo

TALKING POINT

Which of the following do you think makes a book a good thriller or detective story? Refer to any books which you have read or liked.

- short sentences and short chapters
- an exciting ending to each chapter
- an exotic location
- plenty of action
- a simple plot
- plenty of violent murders
- a likeable detective
- romantic interest
- a surprise ending
- authentic background detail

WRITING

Linking devices: contrast

As well as with *but* and *however,* you can express contrast using *although* and *in spite of*. *In spite of* is followed by a noun or a verb in the -*ing* form. It is used when the subject of both the sentences is the same.

EXAMPLE
Although Agatha Christie lived to an old age, the public knew little about her personal life.

In spite of living to an old age, Agatha Christie did not reveal much about her personal life.

1 Rewrite these sentences using *although* or *in spite of*.

1. Carlo suspected Agatha would not return but she waited up anxiously all night.
2. They searched everywhere but they did not find Mrs Christie.
3. Agatha Christie knew about her husband's affair with another woman but she still loved him.
4. Her husband said that she had lost her memory but nobody knows the truth.

2 Write two or three paragraphs about a murder mystery or thriller you have enjoyed reading or watching on TV.

Say where the story takes place and who the main characters are, and give a brief outline of the plot. Also say why you liked the book or film. Try to include a contrasting idea using *although* or *in spite of*.

107

Communication

Expressing regrets

📼 DIALOGUE

STUART: Look at my suit. It's soaked. I wish the office was nearer the station.
LOUISE: Never heard of umbrellas?
STUART: What's the matter with you then?
LOUISE: I feel ghastly. I wish I hadn't gone to bed so late.
STUART: What time did you get to bed?
LOUISE: About two a.m. I watched the late-night movie. I really regret it now.
STUART: You should have recorded it. Haven't you got a video?
LOUISE: No, I wish I had.

Listen and answer the questions.

1 Why is the man soaked?
2 Is the station near the office?
3 What's the matter with the girl? Why?
4 Why didn't she record the film?

FOCUS
Expressing regrets

- Regret about the present:
  I wish the office was nearer the station.
  I wish the office wasn't so far from the station.
  I wish I had a video.

- Regret about the past:
  I wish I hadn't gone to bed so late.
  I wish I'd gone to bed earlier.

Points to note

- When referring to present time, the verb in the main clause is in the past tense:
  I wish the office was nearer the station (but it isn't).
  I wish I had a video (but I haven't).

- When referring to past time, the verb in the main clause is in the past perfect tense:
  I wish I hadn't gone to bed so late (but I did).
  I wish I'd gone to bed earlier (but I didn't).

What's the difference in meaning?

1 I wish he wrote to me occasionally.
2 I wish he had written to me occasionally.

UNIT 48: Communication

PRACTICE

1 Look at the example then complete the sentences in the same way.

EXAMPLE
1 I wish I lived nearer town . . .
  I wish I lived nearer town but I don't.

2 I wish I was good at tennis . . .
3 I wish I'd brought some warmer clothes . . .
4 I wish I hadn't lent her my bike . . .
5 I wish I didn't live in the country . . .
6 I wish I could speak German . . .

2 Work in pairs. Make a list of things you don't like about yourself and your present situation.

Think about your job, your studies, your friends and social life, your home life, your appearance, your abilities and your daily routine.

3 Now talk about your present life.

EXAMPLE   SOCIAL LIFE:
           I wish I had a car.

4 What things in your past life do you regret? Rewrite the regrets below as full sentences using *I wish* and the past perfect tense.

EXAMPLE
1 not working harder at school.
  I wish I'd worked harder at school

1 not working harder at school.
2 giving up piano lessons.
3 not reading more books.
4 not taking up acting.
5 not getting to know my grandparents better before they died.
6 not travelling when I had the opportunity.
7 going straight into work from school.
8 spending all my money on records and clothes.

LISTENING

Listen to a young man talking about his university career. What does he regret about his education so far? Listen again and note the different ways in which he expresses these regrets. Expand the notes into sentences starting with: *He wishes he* . . .

WRITING

Write a simple short story starting with one of the following lines.
I wish I had never . . . bought the piano.
                        invited Carlos home.
                        put the advertisement in the paper.
                        decided to take riding lessons.
                        taken the short cut to work.

Start like this:
I wish I had never decided to take riding lessons. It all started like this . . .

TALKING POINT

What do you think is happening in the picture below?

What social changes in your surroundings do you feel sorry about?

EXAMPLE
I wish they hadn't destroyed the old railway station/
built the new shopping centre/
changed the colour of the telephone boxes.

49

Grammar

Third conditional *if* clauses

Speech bubbles (from photo):
- I only parked here for a few minutes.
- Yes, but you're on a double yellow line. If you'd parked on a meter, you wouldn't have got a ticket.
- If there hadn't been a queue at the bank, I'd have got back before she caught me.

Answer the questions.

1 Did the woman park on a meter?
2 Did the traffic warden give her a parking ticket?
3 Why didn't she get back earlier?

What's the difference in meaning?

1 If you parked on a meter, you wouldn't get a ticket.
2 If you'd parked on a meter, you wouldn't have got a ticket.

What does *'d* stand for in the second sentence? What differences are there in the verb tenses in these sentences?

> **FOCUS**
>
> **The third (or past) conditional**
>
> This structure is used
> - to imagine consequences of things that did not happen in the past:
>   *If you'd (had) parked on a meter, you wouldn't have got a ticket.*
>   (You didn't park on a meter so you got a ticket.)
>   *If there hadn't been a queue at the bank, I'd have (would have) got back before she caught me.*
>
> **Points to note**
> - *Would have* never occurs in the *if* clause.
> - *Might have* or *could have* are used instead of *would have* if the consequence is less definite:
>   *If you'd asked me earlier, I might have been able to help.*

UNIT 49: Grammar

PRACTICE

1 Join each pair of sentences to make one sentence in the third conditional.

EXAMPLE
1 I borrowed the money.
  I was able to buy the bike.

  If I hadn't borrowed the money, I wouldn't have been able to buy the bike.

2 I didn't catch the bus.
  I was late for work.
3 I watched the late-night film on television. I overslept.
4 I didn't work hard at school. I didn't get to university.
5 We couldn't find a baby-sitter. We didn't go out.
6 She went out with wet hair. She caught a cold.

2 Write new sentences using a third conditional and the words in brackets.

EXAMPLE
1 I'm glad you reminded me about Jack's birthday. (forget)

  If you hadn't reminded me about Jack's birthday, I'd have forgotten about it.

2 If only I'd left earlier! (miss train)
3 I wish I'd taken more money with me. (buy that jacket)
4 Why did I eat so much last night! (feel so awful today)
5 It's a good thing that you were wearing seatbelts. (may get hurt)
6 Unfortunately the car broke down. (go to the party)

LISTENING

Listen to two people talking about an incident which happened recently in London involving a businessman and a taxi driver. Answer the questions.

1 What was the businessman carrying?
2 Where had he been?
3 Where did he get out of the taxi?
4 What did he discover and what did he do about it?
5 What did the taxi driver do?

TALKING POINT

1 What would you have done if you'd been the taxi driver?
2 How could the taxi driver have 'vanished into thin air'?
3 What would you have asked or said to the businessman if you'd been the policeman in charge of the incident?

Doctor saves man in Jet Drama

SIXTY-FIVE-YEAR-OLD Mr Ivan Kowalski had a lucky escape yesterday when he collapsed from lack of oxygen on a flight to Warsaw.

The British Airways Tristar en route to Warsaw had been flying steadily at 30,000 feet when it suddenly flew into a storm.

According to flight attendant Marie Parks: 'It was extremely bumpy. Even the crew had to strap themselves in.'

Mr Kowalski, who was on his way to visit relations in Poland, said: 'I felt a sudden pain in the chest and couldn't breathe. It was very frightening indeed. I was lucky there was a doctor on board.'

Said 43-year-old Canadian doctor, Peter Jenkins: 'I only did what any other doctor would do. It was a very turbulent flight.

The man had obviously panicked and the panic had brought on a bad attack of asthma. Fortunately there is always oxygen on board for this type of emergency.'

READING

1 Read the newspaper article and answer the questions.

1 Who had a lucky escape?
2 What happened and why?
3 Who helped him and how?

2 Complete the sentences using the information from the news item.

1 The flight wouldn't have been so bumpy if . . .
2 If Mr Kowalski hadn't panicked, . . .
3 Mr Kowalski might have died if . . .
4 The doctor wouldn't have been able to help him if . . .

WRITING

Either write a short news story with the headline: BOY SAVED IN DRAMATIC HELICOPTER RESCUE or write about another dramatic incident which might have had tragic consequences if certain actions had not been taken.

Use the text about Mr Kowalski as a guide for your writing. Say who was involved in the incident and where it took place. Say briefly what happened and end your news story with a sentence starting with If . . .

50

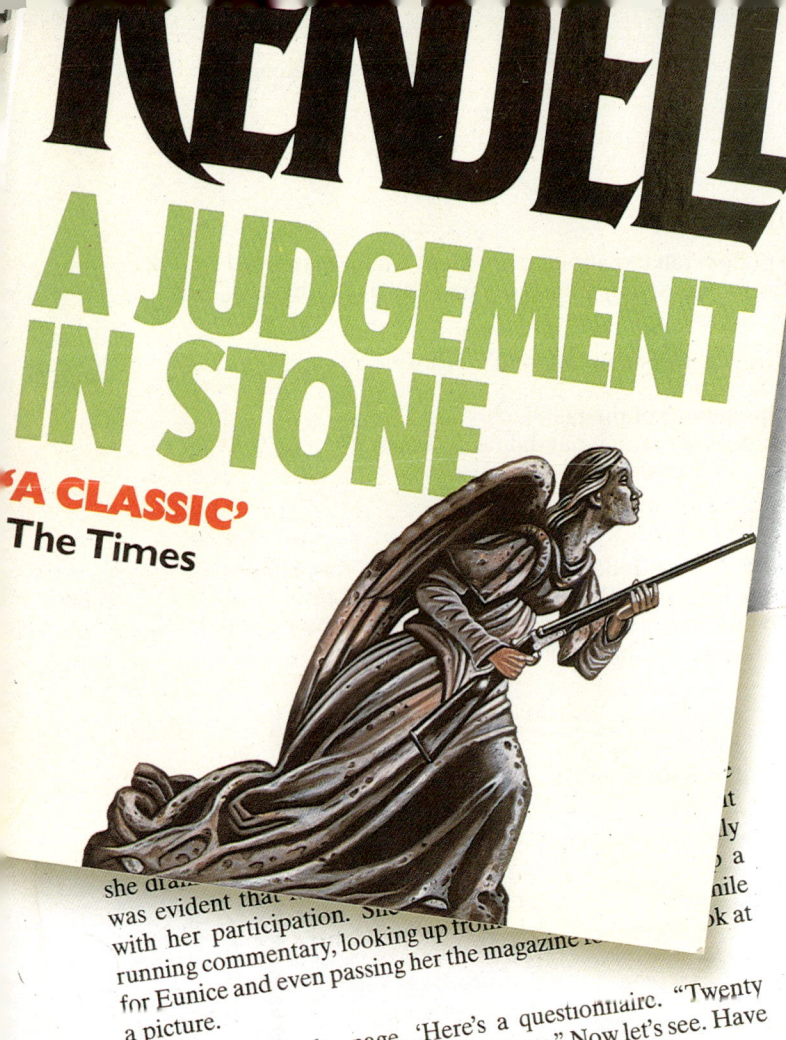

Reading

A JUDGEMENT IN STONE
by Ruth Rendell

If the Coverdales had not been so desperate for help, they would never have employed Eunice Parchman for the job as housekeeper. And if they hadn't been so kind to her, Eunice would never have hated them so much. And if they hadn't discovered her terrible secret, she might never have murdered them…

🔲 LISTENING

Listen to an extract from a radio programme about the latest crime books. The panel are discussing *A Judgement in Stone* by Ruth Rendell.

Note:
1 what Eunice's terrible secret was.
2 why the book is unusual.

The extract on the left from the novel describes how Eunice's secret is revealed to the daughter of the house.

Guess the meaning
puzzled   flushed   blank
vaguely   disease

…she drained… was evident that… with her participation. She… running commentary, looking up from… for Eunice and even passing her the magazine to… a picture.

Melinda turned the page. 'Here's a questionnaire. "Twenty Questions to Test if You're Really in Love." Now let's see. Have you got a pencil or pen or something?'

A firm shake of the head from Eunice.

'I've got a pen in my bag.' Eunice, watching her fetch it, hoped she would take bag, pen and magazine elsewhere, but Melinda returned to her place at the table. 'Now, "Question One: Would you rather be with him than…" Oh I can see the answers at the bottom, that's no good, I'll tell you what, you ask me the questions and tick if I get three marks or two or none at all. O.K.?'

'I haven't got my glasses,' said Eunice.

'Yes, you have. They're in your pocket.'

And they were. The tortoise-shell ones. The pair the Coverdales knew as her reading glasses. Eunice didn't put them on. She did nothing for she didn't know what to do. She couldn't say she was too busy. Too busy for what?

Melinda reached across and picked the glasses out of her pocket. Eunice made no move to take them. She was trying to think. What to do, how to get out of it. Puzzled, Melinda let her hand fall, and as she did so, she looked through the glasses from a short distance and saw that they were of plain glass. Her eyes went to Eunice's flushed face, her blank stare, and pieces of the puzzle — the way she never read a book, looked at a paper, left a note, got a letter — fell into place.

'Miss Parchman,' she said quietly, 'are you dyslexic?'

Vaguely, Eunice thought this must be the name of some eye disease.

'Pardon?' she said hopefully.

'I'm sorry. I mean you can't read, can you? You can't read or write.'

UNIT 50: Reading

COMPREHENSION
Answer the questions.

1 What did Melinda find in her magazine?
2 Why did Eunice give 'a firm shake of the head'?
3 What did Melinda want Eunice to do?
4 How did Eunice try to avoid doing it?
5 Was this true?
6 How did Melinda find out that Eunice's glasses weren't real?
7 What other clues made Melinda suspect that Eunice was dyslexic?

THINK ABOUT IT

1 Why did Eunice keep the glasses in her pocket?
2 Why do you think Eunice's face was flushed?

TALKING POINT

1 If you had been Eunice, how would you have avoided doing the questionnaire?
2 Imagine that you couldn't read or write. How would it affect your daily life? What sort of things would you be unable to do and enjoy?
3 What sort of help can be given to people who are dyslexic?

STYLE

Some of the sentences in the text are not complete sentences. They have no main verbs.

EXAMPLE
A firm shake of the head by Eunice.

This has the effect of making the narrative more dramatic. How many more examples of sentences without main verbs can you find? What are the missing parts of the sentence in each case?

VOCABULARY

An adverb is often used after the verb *said* to describe the way something is spoken.

EXAMPLE
'Miss Parchman,' she said quietly.

1 Write adverbs from the following adjectives.

nervous   suspicious   rude   angry   enthusiastic   hopeful

2 Now select the correct adverb to complete the following.

1 'I don't care who you are,' she said . . .
2 'Perhaps she'll be on the next train,' she said . . .
3 'Get out of here,' he said . . .
4 'Is it my turn now?' he asked . . .
5 'We've got a terrific timetable this term,' said the girl . . .
6 'What have you put in here?' she asked . . .

3 Adverb stress

Listen and repeat the adverbs. Notice where the main stress falls and write it in capital letters.

EXAMPLE
nervously   NERVously

WRITING

1 Rewrite the following two paragraphs from *A Judgement in Stone* inserting the correct punctuation and capital letters.

the silence endured for a full minute melinda too had blushed why didnt you tell us she said as eunice got up wed have understood lots of people are dyslexic i did a study of it in my last year at school Miss Parchman shall i teach you to read im sure it could be fun i could begin in the easter holidays

eunice took the two mugs and set them on the draining board she stood still with her back to melinda then she turned round slowly and fixed melinda with a stare if you tell anyone im what you said ill tell your dad youve been going with that boy and youre going to have a baby

2 In pairs or individually, use your imagination to write the next 200 words of the book.

Imagine what Melinda said in reply and how the dialogue continued. What do you think they did after they had finished talking?
Make sure you punctuate any dialogue correctly. Read your versions out to each other afterwards.

Self check 5

Units 41-50

YOUR HANDS WILL REVEAL YOUR CHARACTER AND LIFE PATTERN.

DR. LINDSAY
D.M.S. ASTRAL

Your personal horoscope individually interpreted in detail. Phone 0772 58623 for an appointment.

1 You go to see Dr Lindsay. Report what he told you.

1 'One of your relatives is ill in hospital.'
2 'You have been worrying a lot lately.'
3 'A friend of yours has just had a baby.'
4 'You received an important letter last week.'
5 'You are going to travel abroad next summer.'
6 'You will meet and fall in love with a stranger.'
7 'I can see a wedding in your life.'
8 'You are improving at English.'

2 Report the questions you asked Dr Lindsay.

1 'What can you see in my palm?'
2 'What are my career chances?'
3 'How long am I going to live?'
4 'Have I got any hidden health problem?'
5 'Where will I be next year?'
6 'When am I going to get married?'
7 'Did I pass my exam yesterday?'
8 'Are my parents going to move house?'

3 Choose from the verbs of reporting below to complete the sentences.

invite   refuse   suggest   apologise   promise   remind   tell   warn

1 'Tomorrow's class is cancelled.'
   (The teacher/us)
2 'Would you like to come to the café with us?'
   (She/me)
3 'I can't let you into the match without a ticket.'
   (The man/them)
4 'I'm sorry I shouted at you.'
   (He/her)
5 'I'll phone this evening. Don't worry.' (She . . .)
6 'Don't forget to double-lock the front door.' (The caretaker/them)
7 'Let's buy her a bunch of white roses.' (He . . .)
8 'I wouldn't cycle on the main road if I were you.' (She/him)

4 Write regrets about your recent visit to Britain, starting with *I wish*.

1 'I didn't go to Scotland.'
2 'I didn't know about the Edinburgh festival.'
3 'I didn't have time to see a typical English village.'
4 'I stayed with our group all the time.'
5 'I didn't take my camera.'
6 'I didn't manage to get a ticket to see "Phantom of the Opera."'

5 Match the two halves of the sentences.

1 They would have got better exam results
2 She would have gone to California
3 If you'd told me the date of her birthday
4 I would have bought a new suit
5 If I hadn't missed the turning
6 If I'd known about her accident
7 If you'd warned me about the mosquitos
8 The house might have caught fire

a) if I'd known about the sale.
b) I wouldn't have got lost.
c) I would have visited her in hospital.
d) I wouldn't have camped by the lake.
e) if she hadn't smelt burning.
f) if she'd got that American job.
g) if they'd studied a bit harder.
h) I would have sent her a card.

6 Read the following situations and write sentences with *if*.

1 I didn't know you needed the eggs for the cake. I used them all.
2 She went to Mexico. She met her future husband.
3 You didn't take my advice. You lost your wallet.
4 He didn't send off the form in time. He didn't get a prize.
5 She hurt her ankle. She didn't win the match.
6 It was foggy. I arrived late.

7 Choose the correct response.

1 A: Good luck on Monday!
   B: a) Yes, I will.
      b) And to yours.
      c) Thanks a lot.

2 A: Bye bye, and don't get sunburnt.
   B: a) Thanks, I'll need it.
      b) Don't worry, I won't.
      c) The same to you.

3 A: Have a nice weekend!
   B: a) Thanks and the same to you.
      b) Don't worry, I won't.
      c) I really must be going.

4 A: Give my regards to your family.
   B: a) No, I won't.
      b) Thanks, I will.
      c) Goodbye.

8 What would you say in the following situations?

1 A colleague indicates that she wants to speak to you while you are talking to someone on the phone.
2 Your doorbell rings while you are in the middle of a telephone conversation with a friend.
3 You meet an ex-colleague from work in the street during your lunch hour. You would like to meet them again.
4 You say goodbye to some friends who are going on holiday.

Fluency 5

Pupils in Terror Ride

By PAUL SMITH

THE DRIVER of a double-decker school bus was being questioned by police yesterday after parents had complained that he had taken twenty of their children on a high-speed terror ride and left them thirty miles from home.

Eventually a handful of 16-year-olds broke out of the bus and telephoned their parents. They said that because some of them were running up and down the stairs ringing the bell and shouting, the driver got angry. He suddenly slammed the doors shut and accelerated so fast that some of the children fell and hit their heads.

The children claimed he raced through country lanes and took the corners so fast that they were thrown to the floor. Some of the children were in tears and others wrote Help signs on their homework pads and held them against the windows.

Anxious parents telephoned the bus company and the school when their children failed to return at the usual time. Said Mrs Ann Stoker, whose children Caroline, fourteen, and Tom, sixteen, were on the bus, said: 'Anything could have happened. I don't care how naughty the children were, it was quite wrong to drop them thirty miles away from home. Most of the children had no money for another bus or for the phone. I am extremely angry.'

A spokesman for the bus company said: 'We are looking into the matter. The driver was clearly provoked.'

1 A discussion

In groups, discuss these questions.

1 Was the bus driver right to do as he did?
2 What would you have done in his position if you had been provoked by the children?
3 How do you think the children got off the bus?

2 A conversation

Choose one of the following conversations to act out.

1 An anxious parent phones the head teacher to find out why the children haven't arrived home.
2 One of the 16-year-olds who have escaped from the bus phones his/her parents.
3 The bus driver tells his wife the same evening what he did and why.

3 A letter

You are a parent. Write to the head of the school about the incident. Report briefly what your daughter/son said had happened on the bus and ask the head to do something about it.

4 A meeting

The head of the school has called a meeting of teachers and parents to discuss the children's bad behaviour on school buses and public transport, and to decide what can be done about it. Act out the meeting. You are either a teacher or a parent.

5 A game: excuses

Choose a word and write it on a piece of paper. The word may be a noun, verb, adjective or adverb, e.g. *window, knock*. Fold the paper and give it to your teacher. Each student then selects a piece of paper and makes up a leave-taking excuse which includes the word on the paper, e.g. *I really must go. Someone is knocking at the door*. The other students must guess which word was on the paper.

Grammar index

	Example sentence	Unit
A		
after	After joining The Damned, he went to live on his own.	7
allowed to	We're not allowed to go in.	4
already (with present perfect)	I've already done it	22
as . . . as	. . . as separate as the notes of a piano . . .	10
as soon as	I'll phone you as soon as I get home.	16
as well as	She likes watching football as well as playing it.	5
B		
be able to	Although the sea was rough, they were able to swim to the shore.	14
besides	Besides, I enjoy travelling.	31
be used to	I'm used to eating salads.	9
both . . . and	She likes both watching football and playing it.	5
C		
can (ability)	She can sing well.	14
can (+ verbs: remember, understand, smell, hear, feel, taste, see)	I can smell something burning.	14
can't have	She can't have forgotten.	39
causative *have*	I'm having my car serviced on Friday.	34
conditionals	(See first, second and third conditionals.)	
contact clauses	That's the man I was talking about.	29
could (ability)	When I was young, I could dance quite well.	14
(request)	Could you take this to the Computer Centre, please?	13
	Do you think you could hurry?	13
could have	She could have had a late meeting.	39
D		
defining relative pronouns	(See *who, which, that, whose, where*)	
do (contrasted with *make*)	He did his homework.	24
during	He changed his name during one of his tours.	7
E		
expected to	Am I expected to make a speech?	28
F		
first conditional	If it starts to rain, we'll play inside.	16
for (with present perfect)	She's lived here for three years.	22
future tenses	(See *will* and *going to*.)	22
G		
gerund (after time adverb)	After joining The Damned . . .	7
(+ main verb)	He suggested meeting at the rink.	44
(after preposition)	He apologised for being rude.	44
get (+ adjective)	I'm getting tired.	21
(+ past participle)	I got fired.	21
going to future (plan/ intention)	I'm going to ask for a rise.	12
(prediction)	It's going to rain.	12

	Example sentence	Unit
H		
have to	Do I have to wear a jacket?	28
have something done	(See causative *have*.)	
however	We usually stay at home in the summer. However, this year we are . . .	37
I		
I'd like (+ noun phrase + past participle)	I'd like my tyres checked, please.	34
in case	I'll take some coins in case I need to phone.	19
indirect questions	Could you tell me what time the next train leaves, please?	33
	I don't know whether to type it.	38
	I don't understand why they need more information.	38
infinitive (after question words)	I don't know what to say.	38
(in indirect commands)	He warned me not to stay.	44
(+ object + infinitive)	He advised me to leave.	44
-ing form	(See gerund.)	
inversion	So/Nor do I.	1
L		
like (= similar to)	. . . like birds in a nest . . .	10
M		
make (contrasted with *do*)	He made a delicious cake.	24
might have	She might have got the wrong day.	39
modal verbs	(See *can, could, will, should, must, can't have, could have, might have, must have, ought to have, should have*.)	28
must	You mustn't talk loudly in church.	28
must have	He must have left his glasses on the table.	39
N		
negative questions	Isn't there a pool in Lansbury Park?	18
neither . . . nor	Football is neither fun to play nor very exciting to watch.	5
not only . . . but also	We will not only have to build a new (motorway) but also (improve the parking facilities.)	17
O		
ought to have	We ought to have left earlier.	36
P		
passive tenses	Wine is produced in France.	26
	It was directed by Trevor Nunn.	26
	Have you ever been stopped by the police?	26
past continuous	While she was paying, a boy stole her wallet.	6
past perfect	They realised they had left the tickets at home.	46
past simple	She arrived and had breakfast.	6
phrasal verbs (with *run*)	He ran away from the police.	20
present continuous	Nick is playing the guitar.	2
present simple	Nick plays the guitar.	2
present perfect continuous	He's been working in Stratford.	22
present perfect simple	He's worked in Stratford.	22

	Example sentence	Unit
R		
relative pronouns	(See *who, which, that, whose, where.*)	
reported questions	I asked him when we could meet.	42
	She asked if he was ever frightened.	42
reported statements	He said/told me (that) he lived in Bristol.	42
reporting verbs	(See *verbs of reporting.*)	
S		
second conditional	What would you do if you won £100?	32
should	I think we should thank the vicar.	28
should have	You should have been wearing a seatbelt.	36
since (with present perfect)	I've worked here since 1987.	22
supposed to	You're not supposed to block the street.	4
	I'm supposed to be revising.	4
T		
tag questions	The 49 bus goes there, doesn't it?	18
that (relative pronoun)	This is the dog that followed me all over the Lake District.	29
third conditional	If you'd parked on a meter, you wouldn't have got a ticket.	49
time clauses	(See *when* and *as soon as.*)	9
U		
unless	Unless you go now, you'll miss the train.	16
used to (+ infinitive)	I used to eat a lot of red meat.	9
(+ gerund)	I'm used to eating salads.	9
V		
verbs of reporting (+ infinitive)	They agreed to come.	44
(+ *ing* form)	He suggested meeting at the rink.	44
(+ object + infinitive)	He advised me to leave.	44
(+ two objects)	She introduced me to her husband.	44
W		
when	I'll phone you when I get home.	16
where (defining relative pronoun)	This is the village where I stayed.	29
whereas	In New York you can . . . whereas in Britain . . .	34
which (defining relative pronoun)	This is the dog which followed me all over the Lake District.	29
while	(See *past continuous.*)	
who (defining relative pronoun)	This is the baker who gave me some fresh bread.	29
whose (defining relative pronoun)	That's the man whose cauliflowers won first prize.	29
will future (decision)	I'll tell him tonight.	22
(future fact)	Steve will be thirty next birthday.	12
(prediction)	It'll be like Manhattan.	12
wish	I wish I'd worked harder at school.	48
would you mind (request)	Would you mind asking them to call me?	13
Y		
yet (with present perfect)	I haven't done it yet.	22
	Have you done it yet?	22

Communication index

(This index contains all the Focus points from the Communication units.)

		Unit
Agree		
Agreeing	So/Nor do I.	1
	I agree.	1
	I think you're right.	1
Disagreeing	Oh, I don't./Oh, I do.	1
	I'm not sure I agree.	1
	I disagree.	1
	I really don't agree.	1
Agreeing to do things	O.K.	13
	Yes, sure.	13
	Yes, certainly.	13
	Yes, of course.	13
	Yes, I'll do that.	13
Apologise		
Apologising	Sorry.	8
	I'm sorry.	8
	I'm terribly sorry.	8
	I'm awfully sorry.	8
	I really am sorry.	8
Responding to apologies	That's O.K.	8
	That's all right.	8
	Don't worry about it.	8
	Never mind. It's nothing to worry about.	8
	It doesn't matter.	8
Arrange		
Making future arrangements	(Look), we must get together some time.	43
	(Listen), why don't we meet for lunch?	43
	(Look), I'll give you a ring.	43
Ask		
Asking for things	Could I have a receipt?	13
	Do you think I could have a receipt?	13
Asking people to do things	Could you take this to the Computer Centre please?	13
	Do you think you could hurry?	13
	Would you mind asking them to call me?	13
Asking for information politely	Could/Can you tell me what his work number is, please?	33
	Have you any idea when he'll be back?	33
	Do you know if he received a parcel this morning?	33
Asking for explanations	What's a CV?	38
	What does 'VSO' stand for?	38
	What does 'a supporting statement' mean?	38
Asking indirectly for advice and help	I don't know whether to type it or not.	38
	I don't know what to say.	38
Asking for clarification	I don't understand why they need more information about me.	38
Availability		
Asking if things are available	Have you got the latest Simply Red album?	3
	Have you got any records by Simply Red?	3
	Do you have 'Picture Book' by Simply Red?	3
Saying if things are not available	I'm afraid we've sold out.	3
	I'm afraid it's not in stock.	3
	I'm afraid we haven't got any at the moment.	3

Buy

Deciding to buy	Thanks, I'll have it (them).	3
	Yes, I'll take this one (these), please.	3
	I think I'll have this one (these), please.	3
Deciding not to buy	I think I'll leave it, thank you.	3
	Thanks, but it's (they're) not quite what I want.	3

Check

Checking information	Isn't there a pool in Lansbury Park?	18
	The 49 bus goes there, doesn't it?	18
Checking information with suprise	Aren't you supposed to be at school?	18

Complain

Making a complaint	I'm afraid I can't eat this steak. It's almost raw.	23
	I'm sorry but we can't sit here. It's very draughty.	23

Ending

Ending conversations	Well I suppose I ought to get on.	43
	Listen, I really have to/ought to be going now.	43
Giving a reason for ending a conversation	I must get back to work.	43
	I've got some work to do.	43
	It's getting late.	43

Explain

Giving explanations	It stands for 'Voluntary Service Overseas'.	38
	It means something you add to an application form.	38

Leave-taking

	See you soon/next week.	43
	Good luck with the interview/on Monday.	43
	Give my regards to John.	43
	Have a good evening/weekend/time on Monday.	43
	Take care.	43
	Bye (for) now.	43

Obligation

Asking about obligation	Do we have to stay to the end?	28
	Do you think we should take some flowers?	28
	Am I expected to make a speech?	28
	Am I supposed to look happy?	28

Offer

Offering to make amends	I'll let you know next time.	8
	I'll get you another one.	8
	I'd like to replace it for you.	8
	Let me clean it for you.	8

Opinion

Giving an opinion	I think (that) . . .	1
	I honestly think (that) . . .	1
	I don't think (that) . . .	1

Prohibition

Talking about obligation	I think we should thank the vicar.	28
	You're expected to make a speech.	28
	You're supposed to wear a hat.	28
Talking about prohibition	You're not supposed to smoke.	28
	You mustn't/shouldn't talk loudly in church.	28

Regret

Regretting the present	I wish the office was nearer the station.	48
	I wish the office wasn't so far from the station.	48
	I wish I had a video.	48
Regretting the past	I wish I hadn't gone to bed so late.	48
	I wish I'd gone to bed earlier.	48

Request

Requesting action	Could you change it, please?	23
	Would you mind finding out?	23
	I'd be grateful if you could find us another table.	23
	(See also *Ask*.)	

Vocabulary list

(This list contains all the words in the *Guess the meaning*, *Words to learn* and *Vocabulary* sections of the Students' Book. Pronunciation is shown in the system used in the *Longman Dictionary of Contemporary English*. The number following each word indicates the unit in which it first appears. The symbol /ᵢ/ as in /əˈbɪlᵢti/ indicates that these are two alternative pronunciations, e.g. /əˈbɪlɪti/ or /əˈbɪləti/.

A

ability /əˈbɪlᵢti/ **37**
able (v) /ˈeɪbəl/ **37**
academic (adj) /ˌækəˈdemɪk/ **1**
admit /ədˈmɪt/ **7**
adore /əˈdɔːʳ/ **30**
affectionate /əˈfekʃənᵢt/ **30**
afford /əˈfɔːd/ **1**
aggressive /əˈgresɪv/ **31**
alien /ˈeɪliən/ **30**
although /ɔːlˈðəʊ/ **31**
angry /ˈæŋgri/ **50**
annoy /əˈnɔɪ/ **1**
armchair /ˈɑːmtʃeəʳ/ **10**
aromatic /ˌærəˈmætɪk/ **30**
arrogant /ˈærəgənt/ **1**
athletics /æθˈletɪks/ **17**
attic /ˈætɪk/ **7**
autobiography /ˌɔːtəbaɪˈɒgrəfi/ **47**
awful /ˈɔːfəl/ **7**

B

banquet /ˈbæŋkwᵢt/ **15**
beautiful /ˈbjuːtᵢfəl/ **7**
biography /baɪˈɒgrəfi/ **47**
blank /blæŋk/ **50**
block (v) /blɒk/ **27**
block of flats /ˌblɒk əv ˈflæts/ **27**
boarding school /ˈbɔːdɪŋ ˌskuːl/ **1**
bookcase /ˈbʊk-keɪs/ **10**
borough /ˈbʌrə/ **31**
boxing /ˈbɒksɪŋ/ **17**
boycott (v) /ˈbɔɪkɒt/ **17**
bracelet /ˈbreɪslᵢət/ **31**
brains /breɪnz/ **1**
brave /breɪv/ **5**
brilliant /ˈbrɪljənt/ **37**
bring up /brɪŋ ˈʌp/ **11**
brooch /brəʊtʃ/ **31**
browse /braʊz/ **15**
bully /ˈbʊli/ **5**
bungalow /ˈbʌŋgələʊ/ **27**
burglar /ˈbɜːgləʳ/ **41**
burglary /ˈbɜːgləri/ **41**
bursting out /ˌbɜːstɪŋ ˈaʊt/ **10**

C

candle /ˈkændl/ **10**
candlestick /ˈkændl ˌstɪk/ **10**
cap (n) /kæp/ **7**
capability /ˌkeɪpəˈbɪlᵢti/ **37**
care /keəʳ/ **30**
careless /ˈkeələs/ **30**
chase (v) /tʃeɪs/ **41**
commercial /kəˈmɜːʃəl/ **17**
compete /kəmˈpiːt/ **17**
competitive /kəmˈpetᵢtɪv/ **35**
complex /ˈkɒmpleks/ **15**
complicated /ˈkɒmplᵢkeɪtᵢd/ **30**
conformist /kənˈfɔːmᵢst/ **5**
confused /kənˈfjuːzd/ **25**
constantly /ˈkɒnstəntli/ **31**
contradict /ˌkɒntrəˈdɪkt/ **30**
convinced /kənˈvɪnst/ **25**
cooker /ˈkʊkəʳ/ **7**
cottage /ˈkɒtɪdʒ/ **27**
cough /kɒf/ **31**
courier /ˈkʊriəʳ/ **11**
course /kɔːs/ **17**
court /kɔːt/ **17**
crackle /ˈkrækəl/ **10**
crawling /ˈkrɔːlɪŋ/ **21**
crime /kraɪm/ **41**
criminal (n) /ˈkrɪmᵢnəl/ **41**
cruel /ˈkruːəl/ **30**
cuff-links /ˈkʌf ˈlɪŋks/ **31**

D

day school /ˈdeɪ ˌskuːl/ **1**
decide /dɪˈsaɪd/ **37**
decision /dɪˈsɪʒən/ **37**
degree /dɪˈgriː/ **1**
deliver /dɪˈlɪvəʳ/ **11**
demonstration /ˌdemənˈstreɪʃən/ **41**
detached house /dɪˈtætʃt ˈhaʊs/ **27**
detective story /dɪˈtektɪv ˌstɔːri/ **47**
develop /dɪˈveləp/ **11**
dilemma /dᵢˈlemə/ **37**
disease /dɪˈziːz/ **50**
disgusting /dɪsˈgʌstɪŋ/ **7**
district /ˈdɪstrɪkt/ **27**
do someone a favour /duː ˌsʌmwʌn ə ˈfeɪvəʳ/ **21**
dreadful /ˈdredfəl/ **7**
drown /draʊn/ **25**

E

earrings /ˈɪəˌrɪŋz/ **31**
embark /ɪmˈbɑːk/ **15**
emergency /ɪˈmɜːdʒənsi/ **41**
eminent /ˈemɪnənt/ **30**
energy /ˈenədʒi/ **23**
enough /ɪˈnʌf/ **31**
enthusiastic /ɪnθjuːziˈæstɪk/ **50**
essential /ɪˈsenʃəl/ **37**
ethical /ˈeθɪkəl/ **37**
ethnic /ˈeθnɪk/ **15**
evening class /ˈiːvnɪŋ ˌklɑːs/ **1**
exhausted /ɪgˈzɔːstɪd/ **41**
experiment /ɪkˈsperᵢmənt/ **30**
extrovert /ˈekstrəvɜːt/ **5**

F

factory /ˈfæktəri/ **7**
fanatic /fəˈnætɪk/ **11**
fail (an exam) /feɪl/ **1**
fascinate /ˈfæsᵢneɪt/ **31**
fees /fiːz/ **1**
fireguard /ˈfaɪəgɑːd/ **10**
fireplace /ˈfaɪəpleɪs/ **10**
finally /ˈfaɪnəli/ **21**
financial /fᵢˈnænʃəl/ **31**
floodlit /ˈflʌdlɪt/ **27**
flushed /flʌʃt/ **50**
football /ˈfʊtbɔːl/ **17**
fortune /ˈfɔːtʃən/ **1**
fortunate /ˈfɔːtʃənət/ **15**
freedom /ˈfriːdəm/ **1**
funny /ˈfʌni/ **30**

G

get into college /ˌget ɪntə ˈkɒlɪdʒ/ **1**
ghost /gəʊst/ **25**
go to college /ˌgəʊ tə ˈkɒlɪdʒ/ **1**
golf /gɒlf/ **17**
gold chain /ˌgəʊld ˈtʃeɪn/ **31**
go up /gəʊ ˈʌp/ **11**
grade /greɪd/ **1**
grin (n) /grɪn/ **41**
guilty /ˈgɪlti/ **25**
gymnastics /dʒɪmˈnæstɪks/ **17**

H

half-hearted /ˌhɑːf ˈhɑːtɪd/ **37**
handicap /ˈhændɪkæp/ **1**
handle /ˈhændl/ **37**
hard /hɑːd/ **5**
hardworking /ˌhɑːdˈwɜːkɪŋ/ **5**
heart /hɑːt/ **30**
heartless /ˈhɑːtləs/ **30**

helpful /ˈhelpfəl/ 7
home /həʊm/ 30
homeless /ˈhəʊmləs/ 30
hopeful /ˈhəʊpfəl/ 7
house /haʊs/ 27
hurricane /ˈhʌrɪkən/ 30
hut /hʌt/ 27

I
ice rink /ˈaɪs rɪŋk/ 17
ice skating /ˈaɪs ˌskeɪtɪŋ/ 17
ideal (adj) /aɪˈdɪəl/ 17
important /ɪmˈpɔːtənt/ 37
independence /ˌɪndəˈpendəns/ 31
instantly /ˈɪnstəntli/ 27
interesting /ˈɪntrəstɪŋ/ 15
invade /ɪnˈveɪd/ 17

J
job /dʒɒb/ 30
jobless /ˈdʒɒbləs/ 30

K
kind /kaɪnd/ 15

M
mantlepiece /ˈmæntlpiːs/ 10
matting /ˈmætɪŋ/ 10
mess /mes/ 7
motor racing /ˈməʊtə ˌreɪsɪŋ/ 17
mugging /ˈmʌgɪŋ/ 41
murder /ˈmɜːdər/ 25/41

N
necessary /ˈnesɪsəri/ 15
necklace /ˈnekləs/ 31
nervous /ˈnɜːvəs/ 50
nice /naɪs/ 15
noisy /ˈnɔɪzi/ 5
nought /nɔːt/ 31

O
on board /ɒn bɔːd/ 15
off duty /ɒf ˈdjuːti/ 41
office block /ˈɒfɪs ˌblɒk/ 27
old-fashioned /əʊld ˈfæʃənd/ 30
one-bedroom flat /ˈwʌn bedrʊm ˈflæt/ 27
otherwise /ˈʌðəwaɪz/ 1
outstanding /aʊtˈstændɪŋ/ 37
overlooking /ˌəʊvəˈlʊkɪŋ/ 15

P
package /ˈpækɪdʒ/ 11
pain /peɪn/ 30
painless /ˈpeɪnləs/ 30
palace /ˈpæləs/ 27
pass (an exam) /pɑːs/ 1
pass (n) /pɑːs/ 1
patrol (n) /pəˈtrəʊl/ 41
pendant /ˈpendənt/ 31
perceptive /pəˈseptɪv/ 30
persecute /ˈpɜːsɪkjuːt/ 21
pickpocketing /ˈpɪkˌpɒkɪtɪŋ/ 41
piles /paɪlz/ 10
pitch /pɪtʃ/ 17
poison /ˈpɔɪzən/ 25
political /pəˈlɪtɪkəl/ 17
pool /puːl/ 17
popular /ˈpɒpjələ/ 15
possibility /ˌpɒsɪˈbɪlɪti/ 37
power /ˈpaʊər/ 27
prevent /prɪˈvent/ 27
primary school /ˈpraɪməri ˌskuːl/ 1
private school /ˈpraɪvɪt ˌskuːl/ 1
privileged /ˈprɪvɪlɪdʒd/ 1
probability /ˌprɒbəˈbɪlɪti/ 37
procession /prəˈseʃən/ 7
profit /ˈprɒfɪt/ 17
proof /pruːf/ 25
protect /prəˈtekt/ 37
puzzled /ˈpʌzəld/ 50

Q
qualification /ˌkwɒlɪfɪˈkeɪʃən/ 37

R
rape /reɪp/ 41
rebel (n) /ˈrebəl/ 5
recommend /ˌrekəˈmend/ 37
recommendation /ˌrekəmenˈdeɪʃən/ 37
reduce /rɪˈdjuːs/ 5
refined /rɪˈfaɪnd/ 35
refreshing /rɪˈfreʃɪŋ/ 30
reservation /ˌrezəˈveɪʃən/ 37
resilient /rɪˈzɪliənt/ 35
ridiculous /rɪˈdɪkjələs/ 1
ring /rɪŋ/ 17/31
riot /raɪət/ 41
rise (n) /raɪz/ 11
robbery /ˈrɒbəri/ 41
romantic novel /rəʊˈmæntɪk ˈnɒvəl/ 47
rough /rʌf/ 31
rubbish /ˈrʌbɪʃ/ 7
rude /ruːd/ 30
run away from /rʌn əˈweɪ frəm/ 20
run into /ˈrʌn ˈɪntuː/ 20
run out of /rʌn ˈaʊt əv/ 20
run over /rʌn ˈəʊvər/ 20
ruthless /ˈruːθləs/ 35

S
scrape /skreɪp/ 27
scrambling /ˈskræmblɪŋ/ 17
secondary school /ˈsekəndri ˌskuːl/ 1
security /sɪˈkjʊərɪti/ 17
semi-detached house /ˌsemɪdɪˈtætʃt ˈhaʊs/ 27
sensible /ˈsensɪbəl/ 7
shape /ʃeɪp/ 30
shapeless /ˈʃeɪpləs/ 10/30
share /ʃeər/ 7
shoplifting /ˈʃɒpˌlɪftɪŋ/ 41
short stories /ˌʃɔːt ˈstɔːris/ 47
silly /ˈsɪli/ 30
skating /ˈskeɪtɪŋ/ 17
skiing /ˈskiːɪŋ/ 17
skyscraper /ˈskaɪˌskreɪpər/ 27
slope /sləʊp/ 17
smuggling /ˈsmʌglɪŋ/ 41
spectacular /spekˈtækjələr/ 15
spoil /spɔɪl/ 30
stab /stæb/ 25
stand up for himself /stænd ˈʌp fə hɪmˈself/ 5
state school /ˈsteɪt skuːl/ 1
stereotypical /steriəˈtɪpɪkəl/ 30
storm (n) /stɔːm/ 21
street-wise /ˈstriːt ˌwaɪz/ 15
strong /strɒŋ/ 5/37
suffer /ˈsʌfər/ 5
suitable /ˈsuːtəbəl/ 11
superficial /ˌsuːpəˈfɪʃəl/ 30
suspicious /səˈspɪʃəs/ 50
swimming /ˈswɪmɪŋ/ 17
symbol /ˈsɪmbəl/ 27

T
tablecloth /ˈteɪbəlˌklɒθ/ 10
table tennis /ˈteɪbəl ˌtenɪs/ 17
take (an exam) /teɪk/ 1
tall /tɔːl/ 5
tease /tiːz/ 5
tennis /ˈtenɪs/ 17
terraced house /ˌterɪst ˈhaʊs/ 27
terrific /təˈrɪfɪk/ 37
tidy /ˈtaɪdɪ/ 15
theft /θeft/ 41
thriller /ˈθrɪlər/ 47
though /ðəʊ/ 31
thought /θɔːt/ 30
thoughtless /ˈθɔːtləs/ 30
through /θruː/ 31
tired /ˈtaɪəd/ 37
tough /tʌf/ 31
track /træk/ 17
traffic jam /ˈtræfɪk ˌdʒæm/ 11
transform /trænsˈfɔːm/ 30
travel book /ˈtrævəl bʊk/ 47

trod (tread) /trɒd/ **10**
true /tru:/ **30**

U
under pressure
 /ˌʌndəʳ ˈpreʃəʳ/ **5**
unforgettable
 /ˌʌnfəˈgetəbəl/ **15**
unhappy /ʌnˈhæpi/ **15**
universe /ˈju:nəvɜ:s/ **7**
unscrupulous
 /ʌnˈskru:pjʊ̥ləs/ **31**
use /ju:z/ **30**
useless /ˈju:sləs/ **30**
usual /ˈju:ʒuəl/ **15**

V
vaguely /ˈveɪgli/ **50**
vast /vɑ:st/ **17**
volleyball /ˈvɒlibɔ:l/ **17**

W
warehouse /ˈweəˌhaʊs/ **27**
washbasin /ˈwɒʃˌbeɪsən/ **10**
windowsill /ˈwɪndəʊˌsɪl/ **10**
witty /ˈwɪti/ **30**
wonderful /ˈwʌndəfəl/ **7**
wound /wu:nd/ **25**

X
xenophobic /ˌzenəˈfəʊbɪk/ **30**

Self check keys

Units 1–10

Exercise 1
1 he's doing   2 She cycles
3 The children are starting
4 He doesn't like
5 I never work
6 They are travelling
7 she's saying.   8 Do you speak
9 I'm trying
10 She hates working

Exercise 2
buy/bought, go/went, win/won, run/ran, take/took, give/gave, come/came, tell/told, say/said, lose/lost, do/did, make/made, see/saw, bring/brought, speak/spoke, read/read, know/knew,. forget/forgot, steal/stole, find/found

Exercise 3
1 While I was having breakfast
2 When I saw . . . I realised
3 It was raining . . . I woke up.
4 I wrote
5 I took . . . it was raining
6 It was snowing . . .I wanted

Exercise 4
1 I'm not used to
2 Did you use to   3 I'm used to
4 Did you use to
5 I wasn't used to
6 She's used to
7 She didn't use to
8 He's used to

Exercise 5
We have to
we didn't have to
I was allowed to
We're not allowed to
Anyone . . . has to
We're not supposed to

Exercise 6 (Example answers)
1 I enjoy swimming.
2 I have a shower./
   I have breakfast.
3 I'm wearing a white T-shirt and blue jeans.
4 I went to school./
   I bought a magazine./
   I watched television.
5 I was having supper.
6 I used to like playing on the street with my friends.
7 We weren't allowed to chew gum.
8 We're not supposed to speak (Italian) but we sometimes do.

Exercise 7
1 b   2 a   3 a

Exercise 8
1 B 2 E 3 C 4 G 5 A 6 F 7 D

Exercise 9
1 So do I.   2 Nor do I.   3 I do.
4 So do I.   5 I don't.   6 I do.

Exercise 10
(Example responses)
1 Have you got any tickets (left) for (the performance of) Romeo and Juliet tonight?
2 I'm (terribly) sorry I'm late but my alarm clock didn't go off so I missed the bus.
3 I think I'll leave it (thank you). It's not quite what I want. (But thank you for showing it to me.)
4 Don't worry about it. It wasn't valuable (expensive).

Units 11–20

Exercise 1
1 I'm going to do
2 is leaving
3 you're going to like
4 We're going to be
5 Sue and Alan are getting married
6 it's going to snow
7 I'm taking
8 The twins are arriving
9 I'm going to be
10 The new boutique is opening

Exercise 2
1 I'll answer
2 What are you going to do . . . ?
3 I'll get   4 I'll send
5 When are you going to . . . ?/ I'll do
6 I'll turn on   7 I'll have
8 I'm going to/I'll take

Exercise 3
1 she hears/she'll be
2 I won't phone/something important happens.
3 he doesn't come/will you be upset?
4 They'll laugh/they realise
5 you'll like/you meet
6 I'll send/I reach
7 I'll get/they have
8 Will she go/she gets

Exercise 4
1 b   2 e   3 f or i   4 a   5 c   6 h
7 i or f   8 d   9 j   10 g

Exercise 5
1 we can/'ll be able to
2 she can't/she's not able to
3 be able to
4 couldn't/wasn't able to
5 were able to
6 I couldn't/wasn't able to

Exercise 6
1 b   2 b   3 c   4 c   5 a

Exercise 7
(Example responses)
1 Do you think I could leave a message?
   Could you give him/her a message?
   Would you mind taking a message?
2 Could I have/Can I have/ Could you give me/Do you think I could have a receipt, please?
3 Didn't we go to the same school?
   Didn't you go to school with me?
   Weren't you at school with me?
   You went to the same school as me, didn't you?
4 Don't you like ice cream?
5 Do you think you could give me extra grammar lessons?
   Would you mind giving me extra grammar lessons?
6 Aren't you/Weren't you supposed to be at a meeting?
   You're supposed to be at a meeting, aren't you?
   You were supposed to be at a meeting, weren't you?

Units 21-30

Exercise 1
1 break/broke/broken
2 fall/fell/fallen
3 spend/spent/spent
4 steal/stole/stolen
5 bring/brought/brought
6 speak/spoke/spoken
7 spill/spilt/spilt
8 take/took/taken
9 drive/drove/driven
10 see/saw/seen
11 give/gave/given
12 write/wrote/written

Exercise 2
1 When did you buy/I bought
2 What have you done/I've just had
3 Have you ever been/I went
4 Have you seen/When did you have
5 I've already written
6 I've spilt

Exercise 3
1 make 2 done 3 doing
4 make/do 5 made 6 make

Exercise 4
1 C 2 G 3 A 4 D 5 H 6 E
7 F 8 B

Exercise 5
1 are grown 2 is exported
3 are being destroyed
4 was written
5 was assassinated?
6 has not been corrected
7 I've been invited

Exercise 6
1 It's being cooked
2 it's made of
3 It's being repaired
4 Why are the children being sent
5 We're being met

Exercise 7
who which/that which/that
who/which/that which/that

Exercise 8
1 b 2 a 3 b 4 c

Exercise 9
2 5 4 6 1 3

Units 31-40

Exercise 1
1 e 2 c 3 f 4 a 5 b 6 d

Exercise 2
1 didn't know 2 would you give 3 wouldn't wear
4 would get 5 had
6 Would you marry/wouldn't marry was/were

Exercise 3
1 you're not 2 I had to
3 you'll be 4 she apologised
5 you cook 6 I phoned

Exercise 4
1 Have you any idea where John is?
2 Could you tell me how I get to/how to get to the station from here?
3 Can you tell me when the next programme starts?
4 Do you know if we've got any homework?
5 Have you any idea what time the last underground train leaves?
6 Do you know if Sam painted that picture?
7 Could you tell me why everyone is laughing?
8 Can you tell me where the nearest public phone box is?

Exercise 5
1 I'd like my car serviced, please.
2 I'd like this watch repaired, please.
3 I'd like my hair cut, please.
4 I'd like these letters typed, please.
5 I'd like this leather jacket cleaned, please.
6 I'd like all that rubbish taken away, please.

Exercise 6
1 a 2 c 3 c

Exercise 7
1 You should have seen
2 you ought to go
3 You shouldn't have taken
4 We should have thought
5 You ought to write

Exercise 8
1 You shouldn't have kept the change.
2 I shouldn't have got so angry.
3 They should have checked the time of the train.
4 I should have taken my swimming things.
5 He shouldn't have been drinking and driving.

Exercise 9
1 I can't find my keys anywhere. I think I must have lost them.
2 You shouldn't have driven when it was so foggy. You might have had an accident.
3 You never know. They might have taken the wrong bus.
4 She can't have telephoned because I was in all day.
5 I'm glad you didn't come to see me yesterday. You might have caught my cold.
6 I can't have lost my passport. It was here on the table just a few minutes ago.

Exercise 10
1 b 2 c 3 a

Exercise 11
(Example responses)
1 Excuse me, could/can you tell me which platform the next train to Bath leaves from?
2 I'd like this (suede) jacket repaired, please.
3 Could/Can you tell/explain to me what Apex means, please?
4 Could you help me write a speech for my teacher's leaving party?/I don't know what to say in my speech. Could you help me?
5 I don't understand why you want to walk home alone.

Units 41-50

Exercise 1
1 He told me that one of my relatives was ill in hospital.
2 He told me that I had been worrying a lot lately.
3 He told me that a friend of mine had just had a baby.
4 He told me that I had received an important letter the week before.
5 He told me that I was going to travel abroad the following summer.

6 He told me that I would meet and fall in love with a stranger.
7 He told me that he could see a wedding in my life.
8 He told me that I was improving at English.

Exercise 2
1 I asked him what he could see in my palm.
2 I asked him what my career chances were.
3 I asked him how long I was going to live.
4 I asked him if I had (got) any hidden health problem.
5 I asked him where I would be the following year/the year after.
6 I asked him when I was going to get married.
7 I asked him if I had passed my exam the previous day/the day before.
8 I asked him if my parents were going to move house.

Exercise 3
1 The teacher told us that the following day's/the next day's class was cancelled.
2 She invited me to go/come to the café with them.
3 The man refused to let them into the match without a ticket.
4 He apologised for shouting at her.
5 She promised to phone that evening.
6 The caretaker reminded them to double-lock the front door.
7 He suggested buying her/that we should buy her a bunch of white roses.
8 She warned him not to cycle on the main road.

Exercise 4
1 I wish I'd gone to Scotland.
2 I wish I'd known about the Edinburgh festival.
3 I wish I'd had time to see a typical English village.
4 I wish I hadn't stayed with our group all the time.
5 I wish I'd taken my camera.
6 I wish I'd managed to get a ticket to see 'Phantom of the Opera'.

Exercise 5
1 g 2 f 3 h 4 a 5 b 6 c
7 d 8 e

Exercise 6
(Example responses)
1 If I'd known you needed the eggs for the cake, I wouldn't have used them all.
2 If she hadn't gone to Mexico, she wouldn't have met her future husband.
3 If you'd taken my advice, you wouldn't have lost your wallet.
4 If he'd sent off the form in time, he would have got a prize.
5 If she hadn't hurt her ankle, she would have won the match.
6 If it hadn't been foggy, I wouldn't have arrived late.

Exercise 7
1 c 2 b 3 a 4 b

Exercise 8
(Example responses)
1 Look, I'm afraid I really must be going. I've got to get back to work/Someone has just arrived to see me.
2 There's someone at the door. I'm afraid I must go/I'll give you a ring later.
3 Listen, why don't we meet for lunch some time?
4 Have a lovely holiday/time. (Take care!)

Longman Group UK Limited
*Longman House, Burnt Mill, Harlow,
Essex CM20 2JE, England
and Associated Companies throughout the world.*

© Brian Abbs and Ingrid Freebairn 1989
All rights reserved; no part of this publication
may be reproduced, stored in a retrieval system,
or transmitted in any form or by any means, electronic,
mechanical, photocopying, recording, or otherwise,
without the prior written permission of the Copyright
holders.

First published 1989
Fifth impression 1990

Set in Linotronic 300 Versaille 55

Produced by Longman Singapore Publishers Pte Ltd
Printed in Singapore

ISBN 0 582 021316

Illustrated by Andrew Aloof, Nancy Anderson, Helen Charlton, Julie Douglas, Ricardo Güiraldes, Lorraine Harrison, Graham Humphreys, Bruce Hyatt, Dave Micheson, Andrew Oliver, David Parkins, Shari Peacock, Chris Riley.

Acknowledgements

Many people have helped us to produce this book. In particular we would like to thank our publishing team – Gill Negus, Liz Waters, Linda Pearce, Paul Price-Smith, Vanessa Kelly, Martine Parsons and Nola Plano. We are also grateful to Elaine Walker, Steve Elsworth and many others who have read and commented so helpfully on the manuscript in all its various drafts.

Brian Abbs and Ingrid Freebairn, London 1989

The authors and publishers would like to thank the following for their invaluable comments on the manuscript: D'Arcy Adrian-Vallance, Elaine Brown, Vanessa M. Burke, Steve Elsworth, Luciano Mariani, Carmen de Mir, Sandra Possas, Manuel Ramirez, Mary Spratt, Antoniou Trechas, Elaine Walker.

We are grateful to the following for permission to reproduce copyright material;

Andre Deutsch Ltd for adapted extracts from *How To Be an Alien* by George Mikes; the author's agents for adapted extracts from the article 'The Right Stuff: Ethics for The Eighties' by Susan Jacoby in *Cosmopolitan* magazine; the author, Laurie Lee and Chatto & Windus for an adapted extract from *Cider with Rosie*; News International for an adapted version of the article 'Fairness is a Great Strength' by Rennie Fritch from *Today* (2/2/88); Newspaper Publishing plc for various extracts from *The Independent* (4/2/88); The Observer Ltd for adapted extracts from the article 'Room of my own' by Ena Kendell in *The Observer Colour Supplement* (3/2/85); the author's agents for adapted extracts from *A Judgement in Stone* by Ruth Rendell; Virago Press for an adapted extract from *Gather Together in My Name* by Maya Angelou (printed by Virago Press Ltd, 1985) Copyright (c) 1974 by Maya Angelou.

The extract on page 47 is adapted from *The Loneliness of the Long-Distance Runner* by Alan Sillitoe, published by Pan Books Ltd.

We are grateful to the following for permission to reproduce photographic and illustrative material in this book:-

Action Plus Photographic for page 42; Alba Radio Limited for page 57 (top); Andre Deutsch Limited/George Mikes/How To Be An Alien for pages 68 and 69; Aspect Picture Library for page 62; Avon and Somerset Constabulary for page 96 (bottom); Braun Electric (UK) Limited for page 57 (bottom); The British Library Newspaper Library/The Evening News (Home Edition) for page 106; The British Library Newspaper Library/The News Of The World for page 107; Camera Press Limited for pages 7 (top left) and 61 (bottom right); City of Birmingham Public Libraries Department for page 59; Coca-Cola Great Britain for page 61 (bottom left) – Coca-Cola and Coke are registered trademarks of The Coca-Cola Company; David Redfern Photography for page 17 (bottom); Grafton Books for page 112; The Hutchison Library for page 63; The Image Bank for pages 10 (left), 17 (top), 28 and 81 (top and bottom); The J Allan Cash Photo Library for page 51 (bottom right); Kids Family Centre for page 87; The Kobal Collection for page 47; Longman Photographic Unit/Trevor Clifford for pages 9 (top 4), 23, 46, 50, 100, 108, 113 and 114; Magnum Photos Limited for page 104; Methuen London/Norman Thelwell/A Leg At Each Corner for pages 36 and 37; Network Photographers for pages 7 (bottom right) and 38 (middle left and centre); Metropolitan Police – Public Affairs for page 97; New Internationalist Publications/Peter Wingham for page 15; One Day For Life/Search 88 for page 66; Parker Pen UK Limited for page 61 (top right); Penguin Books Limited/Louise Dahl-Wolfe for page 91; The Photographers' Library for page 9 (bottom); Picturepoint Limited for page 61 (top left); Pitkin Pictorials Limited for page 72; The Really Useful Theatre Company Limited for page 60; Rex Features Limited for pages 64 and 82; Robert Harding Picture Library Limited for pages 31 and 38 (middle right); St John Pope for pages 38, 79 (left), 83 and 110; Simmons Bakers Limited/Hatfield House for page 38 (bottom right); Sunday Times London/Louise Gubb for page 90; Telefocus – A British Telecom Photogragh for page 79 (right); The Telegraph Colour Library for page 72; Tony Stone Photo Library – London for page 39; Topham Picture Library for pages 18 and 81 (middle); Twentieth Century Fox/The National Film Archive for page 61 (bottom middle); Government of the United States of America for page 51 (bottom); Volkswagen/Audi (GB) Limited for page 61 (top middle); Wembley Stadium Limited for page 105; Zefa Picture Library (UK) Limited for page 109.

All photographs not listed above were taken by John Ridley.

We are grateful to the following for permission to use their premises for location photography;

Lee Valley Ice Centre, Lea Bridge Road, Leyton, London E10 7GL; Launceston Place Restaurant, Launceston Place, London W8; Arcade Mazda, Palace Approach, Priory Road, London N8; Theatre Royal, Thames Street, Windsor, Berks; Tower Records, Piccadilly Circus, London W1; Westside Gymnasium, Kensington High Street, London W8; Longman Group UK Ltd, 5 Bentinck Street, London W1.